REFLECT

READING & WRITING

TANIA PATTISON

NATIONAL
GEOGRAPHIC
LEARNING

Australia · Brazil · Mexico · Singapore · United Kingdom · United States

National Geographic Learning,
a Cengage Company

Reflect 6 Reading & Writing

Author: Tania Pattison

Publisher: Sherrise Roehr

Executive Editor: Laura Le Dréan

Managing Editor: Jennifer Monaghan

Director of Global Marketing: Ian Martin

Product Marketing Manager: Tracy Baillie

Senior Content Project Manager: Mark Rzeszutek

Media Researcher: Stephanie Eenigenburg

Art Director: Brenda Carmichael

Senior Designer: Lisa Trager

Operations Coordinator: Hayley Chwazik-Gee

Manufacturing Buyer: Mary Beth Hennebury

Composition: MPS Limited

For permission to use material from this text or product, submit all requests online at **cengage.com/permissions**
Further permissions questions can be emailed to
permissionrequest@cengage.com

Student Book ISBN: 978-0-357-44853-3
Student Book with Online Practice: 978-0-357-44859-5

National Geographic Learning
200 Pier 4 Boulevard
Boston, MA 02210

Locate your local office at **international.cengage.com/region**

Visit National Geographic Learning online at **ELTNGL.com**
Visit our corporate website at **www.cengage.com**

Printed in Mexico
Print Number: 01   Print Year: 2021

SCOPE AND SEQUENCE

WRITING	GRAMMAR	CRITICAL THINKING	REFLECT ACTIVITIES
Choose relevant information	Verb forms for describing the past	Consider various perspectives	▶ Explore the role of small businesses in society ▶ Collaborate on a social entrepreneurship idea ▶ Consider the challenges of social entrepreneurship ▶ Evaluate opportunities for social entrepreneurship ▶ **UNIT TASK** Write a descriptive essay about a social enterprise
Summarize an academic text	Direct and indirect quotes and reporting verbs	Compare research to your own experiences	▶ Consider the effects of caffeine consumption ▶ Relate concepts to your own experiences ▶ Evalutate the effects of electronic devices on your life ▶ Apply new information to your life ▶ **UNIT TASK** Write a summary of an academic text
Paraphrase research material	Modals and expressions for advice	Recognize a writer's cultural context	▶ Consider what makes a team successful ▶ Carry out a SWOT analysis for a team ▶ Generate strategies for successful teamwork ▶ Design a plan that requires teamwork ▶ **UNIT TASK** Write an expository essay on teamwork
Describe how something was done	The passive voice to emphasize what's important	Establish priorities	▶ Analyze what drives engineers ▶ Apply engineering concepts ▶ Evaluate engineering achievements ▶ Consider responses to engineering achievements ▶ **UNIT TASK** Write a process essay describing an achievement in engineering

5 WALL ART
ART — page 98

Video: Counter mapping

Reading 1: Painting prehistory

Reading 2: Making a statement, one wall at a time

Distinguish facts from opinions

Prefixes: *con-, col-, com-,* and *cor-*

6 LOST IN TIME
SOCIAL SCIENCE — page 122

Video: Ghost town at the edge of the world

Reading 1: From boom town to ghost town

Reading 2: Lidar

Synthesize information

Using a dictionary: Choosing the correct meaning

7 IT'S HOW WE SAY IT
COMMUNICATION — page 146

Video: How do you prefer to communicate?

Reading 1: The language-thought connection

Reading 2: Communication across cultures

Annotate a text

Collocations: *Take* + noun

8 MAKE THE RIGHT CHOICE
BEHAVIORAL SCIENCE/ETHICS — page 170

Video: Ethical decision making

Reading 1: Ethics in business, travel, and sports

Reading 2: Learning from history's mistakes

Identify arguments and counterarguments

Compound words

WRITING	GRAMMAR	CRITICAL THINKING	REFLECT ACTIVITIES
Write a review	The pronoun *this*	Evaluate evidence for theories	▶ Consider the value of art from the past ▶ Discuss issues around studying early art ▶ Form an opinion about modern street painting ▶ Take a position on street art ▶ **UNIT TASK** Write a review of a creative work
Explain causes and effects	Past modals	Apply the past to the present	▶ Consider why places are abandoned ▶ Explore the potential of a ghost town ▶ Assess your knowledge of your country's history ▶ Imagine further uses of technology ▶ **UNIT TASK** Write a cause-effect essay about an event in history
Compare and/or contrast	Articles to refer to groups	Consider the limitations of research claims	▶ Consider the relationship between language and thought ▶ Evaluate ideas about language and thought ▶ Analyze potential areas of difficulty in communication ▶ Examine reasons for communication breakdowns ▶ **UNIT TASK** Write a compare-contrast essay about communication
Write persuasively on a discussion board	Unreal conditionals	Understand bias	▶ Analyze whether actions are ethical ▶ Evaluate situations and make ethical decisions ▶ Consider ethics in experiments ▶ Apply ethics to an experiment ▶ **UNIT TASK** Write persuasively on an ethical question

CONNECT TO IDEAS

Reflect Reading & Writing features relevant, global content to engage students while helping them acquire the academic language and skills they need. Specially-designed activities give students the opportunity to reflect on and connect ideas and language to their academic, work, and personal lives.

Academic, real-world passages invite students to explore the world while building reading skills and providing ideas for writing.

Each unit starts with a **high-interest video** to introduce the theme and generate pre-reading discussion.

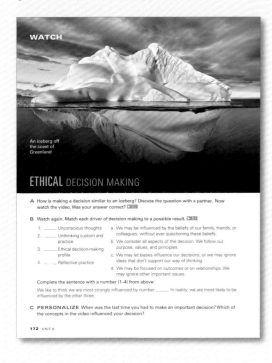

CONNECT TO ACADEMIC SKILLS

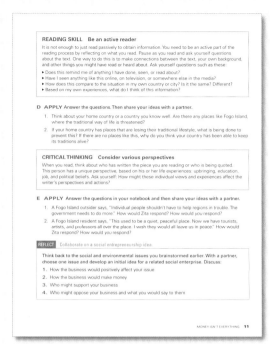

Focused **reading skills** help create confident academic readers.

Reflect activities give students the opportunity to think critically about what they are learning and check their understanding.

Clear writing models and **analyze the model** activities give students a strong framework to improve their writing.

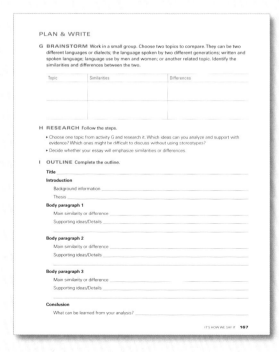

A **step-by-step approach** to the **writing process** along with relevant grammar helps students complete the final writing task with confidence.

CONNECT TO ACHIEVEMENT

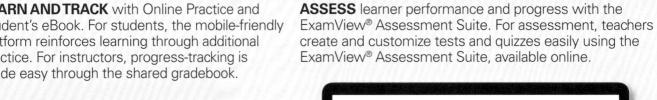

Reflect at the end of the unit is an opportunity for formative assessment. Students review the skills and vocabulary they have gained.

DIGITAL RESOURCES

TEACH lively, engaging lessons that get students to participate actively. The Classroom Presentation Tool helps teachers to present the Student's Book pages, play audio and video, and increase participation by providing a central focus for the class.

LEARN AND TRACK with Online Practice and Student's eBook. For students, the mobile-friendly platform reinforces learning through additional practice. For instructors, progress-tracking is made easy through the shared gradebook.

ASSESS learner performance and progress with the ExamView® Assessment Suite. For assessment, teachers create and customize tests and quizzes easily using the ExamView® Assessment Suite, available online.

ACKNOWLEDGMENTS

The Authors and Publisher would like to acknowledge the teachers around the world who participated in the development of *Reflect*.

A special thanks to our Advisory Board for their valuable input during the development of this series.

ADVISORY BOARD

Dr. Mansoor S. Almalki, Taif University, Saudi Arabia; **John Duplice**, Sophia University, Japan; **Heba Elhadary**, Gulf University for Science and Technology, Kuwait; **Hind Elyas**, Niagara College, Saudi Arabia; **Cheryl House**, ILSC Education Group, Canada; **Xiao Luo**, BFUS International, China; **Daniel L. Paller,** Kinjo Gakuin University, Japan; **Ray Purdy**, ELS Education Services, USA; **Sarah Symes,** Cambridge Street Upper School, USA.

GLOBAL REVIEWERS

ASIA

Michael Crawford, Dokkyo University, Japan; **Ronnie Hill**, RMIT University Vietnam, Vietnam; **Aaron Nurse**, Golden Path Academics, Vietnam; **Simon Park**, Zushi Kaisei, Japan; **Aunchana Punnarungsee**, Majeo University, Thailand.

LATIN AMERICA AND THE CARIBBEAN

Leandro Aguiar, inFlux, Brazil; **Sonia Albertazzi-Osorio**, Costa Rica Institute of Technology, Costa Rica; **Auricea Bacelar**, Top Seven Idiomas, Brazil; **Natalia Benavides**, Universidad de Los Andes, Colombia; **James Bonilla**, Global Language Training UK, Colombia; **Diego Bruekers Deschamp**, Inglês Express, Brazil; **Josiane da Rosa**, Hello Idiomas, Brazil; **Marcos de Campos Bueno**, It's Cool International, Brazil; **Sophia De Carvalho**, Ingles Express, Brazil; **André Luiz dos Santos**, IFG, Brazil; **Oscar Gomez-Delgado**, Universidad de los Andes, Colombia; **Ruth Elizabeth Hibas**, Inglês Express, Brazil; **Rebecca Ashley Hibas**, Inglês Express, Brazil; **Cecibel Juliao**, UDELAS University, Panama; **Rosa Awilda López Fernández**, School of Languages UNAPEC University, Dominican Republic; **Isabella Magalhães**, Fluent English Pouso Alegre, Brazil; **Gabrielle Marchetti**, Teacher's House, Brazil; **Sabine Mary**, INTEC, Dominican Republic; **Miryam Morron**, Corporación Universitaria Americana, Colombia; **Mary Ruth Popov**, Ingles Express, Ltda., Brazil; **Leticia Rodrigues Resende**, Brazil; **Margaret Simons**, English Center, Brazil.

MIDDLE EAST

Abubaker Alhitty, University of Bahrain, Bahrain; **Jawaria Iqbal**, Saudi Arabia; **Rana Khan**, Algonquin College, Kuwait; **Mick King**, Community College of Qatar, Qatar; **Seema Jaisimha Terry**, German University of Technology, Oman.

USA AND CANADA

Thomas Becskehazy, Arizona State University, AZ; **Robert Bushong**, University of Delaware, DE; **Ashley Fifer**, Nassau Community College, NY; **Sarah Arva Grosik**, University of Pennsylvania, PA; **Carolyn Ho**, Lone Star College-CyFair, TX; **Zachary Johnsrud**, Norquest College, Canada; **Caitlin King**, IUPUI, IN; **Andrea Murau Haraway**, Global Launch / Arizona State University, AZ; **Bobbi Plante**, Manitoba Institute of Trades and Technology, Canada; **Michael Schwartz**, St. Cloud State University, MN; **Pamela Smart-Smith**, Virginia Tech, VA; **Kelly Smith**, English Language Institute, UCSD Extension, CA; **Karen Vallejo**, University of California, CA.

MONEY ISN'T EVERYTHING

Ron Finley teaches urban communities to grow their own food.

THURSDAY
STREET CLEANING

2 HOUR
PARKING
8AM–6PM
EXCEPT SUNDAY

CONNECT TO THE TOPIC

1. Why do you think Finley is teaching urban communities to grow their own food?

2. If you could have your own business, what would it be?

WATCH

This bakery in Bogotá, Colombia, provides training and jobs for young people who face barriers to employment.

SOCIAL ENTERPRISE 101

A What do you think a "social enterprise" is? Choose the best definition. Then watch the video and check your answer. ▶ 1.1

a. A business that plans weddings and parties

b. A business that is fun to work at

c. A business that tries to solve social problems

B Watch again and answer the questions. ▶ 1.1

1. What might these businesses do? Match the two sentence parts.

   A bakery might _____   a. bring people in the community together.

   An orchestra might _____   b. help homeowners to reduce costs.

   An environmental company might _____   c. provide training in job skills.

2. What did each person do, and why? Draw lines to form complete sentences.

Akram	started a cafe	to encourage healthy eating in cities.
June	started a garden	to bring young and old people together.
John	started a home-care company	to provide jobs for people with disabilities.

3. What is needed to establish a social enterprise? Discuss.

PREPARE TO READ

A VOCABULARY Complete the sentences with the correct words.

collaboration (n)	ethical (adj)	initiative (n)	preservation (n)	pursue (v)
entrepreneur (n)	facilitate (v)	lucrative (adj)	prosperity (n)	revitalize (v)

1. Lara is concerned about poverty and wants to _____ a career in social work.

2. The _____ of traditional cultures is important; their languages and customs should not be allowed to disappear.

3. As a(n) _____ business, Fair Bean Coffee pays its workers a good wage.

4. A successful _____ requires trust and understanding between partners.

5. Ben has a(n) _____ career as an executive in the oil industry, but he would prefer a job where he helps people, even if he makes less money.

6. The new company created over 500 jobs and helped to _____ the town's economy.

7. June's cafe was a(n) _____ designed to increase employment among people with disabilities.

8. Conrad is a true _____! As a child, he sold homemade lemonade; as a teenager, he designed an app; and as an adult, he established an online bookstore.

9. The city is enjoying a period of economic _____; companies are making profits, and there are plenty of jobs.

10. If you are looking for a new job, the Internet can _____ your search by providing job listings and interview tips.

B PERSONALIZE Discuss these questions with a partner.

1. Would you like to be an **entrepreneur** and start your own business? Explain.

2. What is more important to you when choosing a career—working in a **lucrative** field, helping society, or being creative? Explain.

3. Can you think of a place in your area where the economy has been **revitalized**, or needs to be revitalized, by new businesses?

REFLECT Explore the role of small businesses in society.

You are going to read about an entrepreneur with a social mission. Discuss these questions in a small group.

1. Which group in society you would like to help, or which environmental issue are you most concerned about?

2. How can small businesses and individual entrepreneurs help to solve the problem?

3. What challenges might small businesses encounter when trying to address problems in society?

A BUSINESS CLOSE TO HER HEART

🔊 1.1 *Former oil company worker Zita Cobb has turned her back on the corporate world to pursue her own cultural, artistic, and environmental goals.*

1   On tiny Fogo Island, off the rocky coast of Newfoundland, Canada, Zita Cobb surveys the art studios she has built. Located on the eastern edge of Canada, Fogo Island is home to fewer than 3,000 people. On the 45-minute ferry ride to the island, you might see a whale surfacing or an iceberg floating by. After arriving, you'll see brightly colored houses, enjoy the scenery from the cliffs, and search for crabs in rock pools. You can finish the day staring at star-filled skies free of light pollution from bright buildings. After a career working in the oil industry, Zita has returned to her beautiful home on Fogo Island to build a business close to her heart.

A PREVIEW Answer the questions.

1. Look at the photo and read the first paragraph. What do you think Zita Cobb wants to do?

2. What kinds of improvements or initiatives could benefit Fogo Island?

2   Zita is one of a growing number of people who have left the corporate world in order to **pursue** their own business dreams. Motivated by a creative urge or by a desire to help society or the environment, Zita says the modern **entrepreneur** "serves the needs of culture and the environment and not just business." Zita calls this "a kind of social entrepreneurship, having the very best tools from the traditional, for-profit business world but serving the right ends."

3   Zita's mission was personal: to ensure the **preservation** of Fogo Island's culture and to bring economic **prosperity** back to the island, the place where her ancestors had lived for eight generations. Life on Fogo has always been hard. For many generations, the island lacked roads and electricity. Islanders have traditionally made their living fishing, primarily for cod. When cod stocks became depleted in the 1990s as a result of industrial overfishing, the government issued a moratorium[1] on cod fishing. Many families turned either to government assistance or to **lucrative** jobs elsewhere in Canada; Zita refers to such people as "economic refugees." She says, "As this happens, a little bit of us dies." She regrets that many young Newfoundlanders have been to Disneyland but have never seen a fishing boat.

---

[1]**moratorium** (n) an official order to stop an activity

Squish Studio is one of several art studios on Fogo Island built by Zita Cobb's foundation. One of the foundation's goals is to preserve the island's traditions and culture.

4   As an islander, Zita wanted to **revitalize** the island's economy and encourage the development of the arts and tourism. The result was the Shorefast Foundation[2], established in 2006 with her brothers. About the foundation, Zita says, "We exist in relationship to the whole; the whole planet, the whole of humanity, the whole of existence. Our job is to find ways to belong to the whole while upholding[3] the specificity of people and place."

5   One of the first **initiatives** of the foundation was its arts program. Zita says, "Art-making is thinking, and the power of art is evident in its capacity to translate, enrich, and deepen our experience of the world." To this end, Zita established art studios and an artist-in-residence program; this program enables artists, musicians, and writers from around the world to come to Fogo for a few weeks or a few months. They create, give talks, display their work, and interact with the islanders. When they leave, they become ambassadors for the island.

6   The foundation's initiatives have grown over the years. The New Ocean Ethic runs lectures and research projects designed to explore the island's relationship with the ocean and the effects of climate change. Geology at the Edge is a community-based geology program which provides lectures and youth programs related to the island's geology. In **collaboration** with Newfoundland's Memorial University, Shorefast brings professors and other academics to the island to explore Fogo's culture. The Shorefast Business Assistance Fund offers loans to small businesses on the island to help generate employment. Fogo Island Fish **facilitates** the selling of fish caught the traditional way—with a line and a hook—to restaurants across Canada and ensures a fair price for the fishers.

---

[2]**foundation** (n) an organization that raises money for a social or cultural purpose

[3]**uphold** (v) to maintain; to keep in place

7   At the heart of all of Shorefast's activities is the 29-room Fogo Island Inn, built with the help of donations and with expertise from local craftspeople. Built on the principle of respect for nature and culture, the inn offers an opportunity for visitors to interact with the local islanders and to escape their busy lives. Visitors can go hiking, take a boat trip, hear local music, and get to know locals, enjoying Fogo's traditions. Zita believes that all businesses can be community businesses. As well as providing jobs for local people, she invests 100 percent of the profits from the inn back into the community. There are no investors looking to profit from the inn; the business is for the islanders.

8   In rebuilding Fogo Island's economy and preserving its heritage, Zita sees herself as a new kind of entrepreneur. She is not alone. Around the world, people are choosing unusual careers, often with a cultural or environmental goal. In Mexico, biologist, photographer, and travel writer Katherina Audley established the Whales of Guerrero Research Project, a community-driven research, education, and training program. In Morocco, Dounia Bounahmidi develops **ethical** partnerships with local craftspeople to create home furnishings for her business, Folks & Tales. And in the United States, Rebecca Hui started Roots Studio, which digitizes the work of artists from geographically isolated regions; the works are then entered into an online library that can be used for stationery, clothing, and other products. Rebecca's team has worked with over 3,000 artists around the world.

9   Back on Fogo Island, Zita Cobb has made huge steps in bringing her home community back to life. While social entrepreneurship is not an easy path to choose, those who are able to follow their dreams can enjoy both career satisfaction and the knowledge that they are creating something with deep meaning. As Zita says, "Everything starts with believing."

The Fogo Island Inn

B MAIN IDEAS Answer the questions.

1. What did you learn about Zita Cobb?

   a. She is a businesswoman who used her skills to make a difference in her community.

   b. She is a talented artist who needed a studio to create and display her works of art.

   c. She is a lover of history who thinks the government's policy on fishing was wrong.

2. What lesson can be learned from this reading?

   a. It is important for people to stay in their home communities rather than go elsewhere.

   b. It is possible to make a living and do good in the world at the same time.

   c. Places such as Fogo Island need to face the future and move past their traditional lifestyles.

C DETAILS Choose the correct word or phrase to complete each sentence.

1. Fogo Island is in _____.

   a. the United States   b. England   c. Canada

2. In the past, most islanders made their living from _____.

   a. fishing   b. tourism   c. the oil industry

3. Life became hard for the islanders in the 1990s because of the lack of _____.

   a. government support   b. fish   c. electricity

4. For Zita Cobb, _____ is a way to increase our understanding of the world.

   a. art   b. travel   c. going to college

5. The New Ocean Ethic explores the island's relationship with the ocean and the effects of _____.

   a. geology   b. academics   c. climate change

6. Zita is working with Memorial University to increase understanding of Fogo Island's _____.

   a. culture   b. economy   c. geology

7. Fogo Island Fish ensures _____ for traditional fishers.

   a. enough fish   b. a fair price   c. more fish sales

8. The Fogo Island Inn was largely financed by _____.

   a. investors   b. the government   c. donations

9. If you visit the Fogo Island Inn, you can _____.

   a. swim in the pool   b. hear local music   c. have a beauty treatment

10. Careers with cultural or environmental goals are _____.

    a. unique to Canada   b. not yet established   c. meaningful

READING SKILL   Be an active reader

It is not enough to just read passively to obtain information. You need to be an active part of the reading process by reflecting on what you read. Pause as you read and ask yourself questions about the text. One way to do this is to make connections between the text, your own background, and other things you might have read or heard about. Ask yourself questions such as these:

▸ Does this remind me of anything I have done, seen, or read about?
▸ Have I seen anything like this online, on television, or somewhere else in the media?
▸ How does this compare to the situation in my own country or city? Is it the same? Different?
▸ Based on my own experiences, what do I think of this information?

D APPLY Answer the questions. Then share your ideas with a partner.

1. Think about your home country or a country you know well. Are there any places like Fogo Island, where the traditional way of life is threatened?

2. If your home country has places that are losing their traditional lifestyle, what is being done to prevent this? If there are no places like this, why do you think your country has been able to keep its traditions alive?

CRITICAL THINKING   Consider various perspectives

When you read, think about who has written the piece you are reading or who is being quoted. This person has a unique perspective, based on his or her life experiences: upbringing, education, job, and political beliefs. Ask yourself: How might these individual views and experiences affect the writer's perspectives and actions?

E APPLY Answer the questions in your notebook and then share your ideas with a partner.

1. A Fogo Island outsider says, "Individual people shouldn't have to help regions in trouble. The government needs to do more." How would Zita respond? How would *you* respond?

2. A Fogo Island resident says, "This used to be a quiet, peaceful place. Now we have tourists, artists, and professors all over the place. I wish they would all leave us in peace." How would Zita respond? How would *you* respond?

REFLECT   Collaborate on a social entrepreneurship idea.

Think back to the social and environmental issues you brainstormed earlier. With a partner, choose one issue and develop an initial idea for a related social enterprise. Discuss:

1. How the business would positively affect your issue
2. How the business would make money
3. Who might support your business
4. Who might oppose your business and what you would say to them

PREPARE TO READ

A VOCABULARY Write each word next to the correct definition.

demographic (adj)	indigenous (adj)	literacy (n)	minority (n)	role model (n phr)
funding (n)	launch (v)	maximize (v)	naive (adj)	sustainable (adj)

1. _____ to start

2. _____ smaller group in a population, such as an immigrant group or people with disabilities

3. _____ original to a particular region

4. _____ using an amount of resources that can be maintained without hurting anything else

5. _____ the ability to read and write

6. _____ related to different categories in a population, such as age, gender, ethnicity, or occupation

7. _____ someone a person might look up to and try to copy

8. _____ money provided or raised for a specific cause

9. _____ lacking in experience or wisdom

10. _____ to use something in the most effective or efficient way

B PERSONALIZE Discuss these questions with a partner.

1. Who were your **role models** as a child? Why did you want to be like these people?

2. What do you think visual **literacy** means? Why might visual literacy be an important skill to develop?

3. If you wanted to establish a small business, where would you look for **funding**?

REFLECT   Consider the challenges of social entrepreneurship.

You are going to read an article about how to become a social entrepreneur. Discuss these questions in a small group.

1. What challenges might young people face in trying to establish a social enterprise?

2. Do you think it is easier or more difficult to start a business now than in the past? Explain.

3. What might be the first steps in launching a social enterprise? What challenges does each present?

SO YOU WANT TO BE A SOCIAL ENTREPRENEUR?

A PREVIEW Skim the reading and answer the questions.

1. What do all the people in the reading have in common?

2. Do you agree with the advice from these entrepreneurs?

Honey bees produce honey and play an important role in the pollination of many flowering food crops.

Zita Cobb says that in following your business dream, "Everything starts with believing." Apart from a vision, what else do you need to make the dream a reality? From honey to handbags, these social entrepreneurs give their advice.

Choose something meaningful to you

1   Think about your own life. What do you believe in? As an African American child, Tony Weaver, Jr. enjoyed watching television, but he did not see himself reflected in any of his favorite superheroes. His skin was darker than theirs, and his hair was a different texture. Tony realized that there was a lack of positive black, male **role models** in the media. This was reinforced later during a volunteer experience with young children: One little boy could not decide what to wear to a costume party, since he did not look like any of his white television heroes.

2   At the age of 20, Tony founded Weird Enough Productions, a comic production company dedicated to creating positive images of black men and other **minority** groups. At the heart of Weird Enough is the UnCommons, a group of superheroes made up of members of ethnic and other minority groups. With every story the company produces, there is a lesson plan for teachers on how to use comics to discuss social issues. Weaver says, "Using media **literacy**, digital literacy, and student voice, we awaken the hero in every classroom."

Determine and share your values

3   What are your company's values? How will you communicate these? Blanche Murray, a member of New Zealand's **indigenous** Maori population, is bringing jobs to her community through her successful Kai Ora Honey business. Blanche's values and beliefs were passed down from her grandmother, Saana, a strong believer in the medicinal benefits of local honey, called Mānuka. Her grandmother also believed in the right of the local Maori population to control their own resources. Blanche reports, "She said, 'let's make sure our people are the ones who own and operate this particular industry up here in the Far North and employ our own. And make sure that our own are contributing positively to our society.'"

4   This message is made clear on Kai Ora Honey's website, which reads, "Our success rests in our ability to **maximize** the influence of our heritage and culture as well as the environmental, social, and economic initiatives that we feel support and protect the community around us." Kai Ora Honey's clients appreciate the fact that the business is family owned and makes use of skills that go back for generations. Blanche says, "They love history, they love traditions, they love the Maori culture."

To keep plastic bottles off beaches and out of the ocean, one social enterprise recycles them into clothing.

Use popular tools to reach your market for free

5   You don't need to spend a lot of money to promote your business—just go online! Jake Danehy was in college and his sister Caroline in high school when they **launched** Fair Harbor Clothing. Jake and Caroline were shocked by the number of plastic bottles they saw littering the beaches near their home. Many of these bottles find their way into the ocean. They decided to turn this waste into a line of **sustainable** clothing. Working with factories that turn plastic into fibers and weave it into clothing, the pair produce stylish swimwear for men, women, and children. Each swimsuit is made from 11 recycled bottles. To date, the company has upcycled more than seven and a half million plastic bottles.

6   The Danehys recognize that technology has played a role in the success of their business. Jake says, "Without much experience, Caroline and I were able to start a global supply chain, while she was in high school." Using the Internet, the pair researched fabrics and factories. They decided to market to millennials[1], their own **demographic** group. They rely heavily on social media to reach their target market. Jake says, "It levels the playing field[2] and gives us the ability to spend our marketing dollars in the most efficient way possible." Their approach is working: Sales have grown by up to 1,000 percent each year.

Seek money from anywhere you can think of

7   You may want to help your community, make honey, or save the oceans—but you still need money to get started. One approach for startups is **funding** through social media, known as crowdfunding. How does this work? You share your idea on a crowdfunding website. You then use your project page to tell as many people as you can think of about your need for money—not only family and friends, but also contacts on social media. These people visit your page, and if they like your idea, they can contribute money. Then they tell their friends, who do the same.

8   Vaishali Umrikar had worked with women's services in India and Australia. Motivated by her experiences, she established The Empowerment Bag, a company designed to provide women with literacy training, sewing skills, and fair employment. After

---

[1]**millenial** (n) someone born between 1981 and 1996

[2]**level the playing field** (v phr) to give everyone the same chance to succeed

coming up with the idea to produce a line of practical and eco-friendly backpacks and schoolbags, Vaishali turned to crowdfunding. Her vision quickly got people's attention. She raised $910 on the first day and $2,250 in the first week. She has now helped 200 women, providing not only jobs but also housing, education, and health care for women and children.

Keep going!

9   What do you do if you have no experience in the business you want to create? That was the case with Ben Conard, who started Five North Chocolate while still in college. As a business student, Ben learned that 2 billion people in the world live on less than $2 a day and that much of the world's cocoa is produced by people, including children, who live in extreme poverty. Ben became involved in the fair trade movement, which ensures that businesses meet strict labor standards, including fairly compensating farmers. Traveling through Ecuador and India, Ben saw firsthand the difference fair trade companies can make to local workers.

10   A chocolate enthusiast, Ben decided to focus on the production of fair trade snack foods, cooking up samples in his college dorm room kitchen. With no background in the food industry, he admitted being "super **naive**" at the beginning. He says, "I have vivid memories of sticking labels until I couldn't feel my fingers and messing up batches of chocolate at 4 a.m. . . . leaving me questioning myself as an entrepreneur and if I was even the right person for the job. I still struggle with that." Despite his moments of self-doubt, Ben never quit and kept learning from his experiences. Eventually, he made Five North Chocolate a successful business and was named one of the Top 10 Biggest Fair Trade Advocates in the World.

11   So if you have a business dream and you want to do more than simply make money, keep these tips in mind. Know what you want, determine your values, use social media to publicize[3] your business, try crowdfunding, and—above all—don't give up. As Ben Conard of Five North Chocolate says, "Every hurdle[4] along the journey eventually becomes a lesson learned."

---

[3]**publicize** (v) to make something known

[4]**hurdle** (n) something that makes an achievement difficult; an obstacle

Fair trade chocolate makers ensure that cocoa farmers are paid fairly.

B MAIN IDEAS Who or what did each of the social entrepreneurs from the reading want to help, and how? Complete the chart.

Social entrepreneur(s)	Cause	Product
Tony Weaver, Jr.		
		Honey
	The ocean	
Vaishali Umrikar		
	Workers' conditions	

C DETAILS Complete each item with information from the passage.

1. Write the initials of each social entrepreneur next to what influenced them to start a business.

   a. _____BM_____ a family member

   b. _____ a childhood experience

   c. _____ something seen while traveling

   d. _____ work experience

   e. _____ a local environmental problem

2. Weird Enough Productions creates positive images of _____
   in comic books which can be used to discuss _____.

3. Kai Ora Honey's customers appreciate Blanche Murray's focus on _____ and
   _____.

4. In the early days, Fair Harbor Clothing used social media to _____.

5. People supported Vaishali Umrikar's business through crowdfunding because _____
   _____.

6. Ben Conard had a positive attitude. For example, he _____,
   and this helped him eventually become successful.

REFLECT Evaluate opportunities for social entrepreneurship.

Discuss these questions in a small group.

1. Which of the social entrepreneurs in the article has beliefs that most closely reflect yours? Would you work for this person's business or start a business like theirs? Explain.

2. Would you ever contribute to a crowdfunding request from a young entrepreneur? What factors might you consider when deciding whether or not to donate?

WRITE

> You are going to write an essay about a socially responsible business. Use the ideas, vocabulary, and skills from the unit.

A MODEL As you've learned, the thesis statement is the main idea of an essay and is usually in the introductory paragraph. The body paragraphs support the thesis, and each one usually has a topic sentence with its own main idea. Read the essay. Underline the thesis statement and the topic sentences of paragraphs 2–4.

Keeping the World Clean and Safe

1   When you pick up a product to clean your kitchen or wash your clothes, do you ever think about what that product is made of? Are you worried about how that product might affect your health or the health of the environment? Chicago-based Kate Jakubas and her husband Mike Mayer asked those questions. The result was Meliora, a company dedicated to producing environmentally friendly cleaning products, laundry detergents, and soaps. In establishing Meliora, these social entrepreneurs have developed a line of products that are safe for both people and the planet.

2   Meliora started because Kate, an environmental engineering student, became interested in the ingredients used in cleaning products. In many cases, the ingredients in the products were not listed on the packaging. She started to research cleaning products, and she was shocked to learn that some ingredients were not safe. She decided to make her own laundry soap using safe ingredients. Kate's friend at the time, Mike, played football and was excited to see how clean his muddy clothes were after washing them with Kate's soap. He realized that Kate had an idea worth sharing. Kate had never thought about becoming an entrepreneur, but after winning her university's Sustainable Enterprise competition in 2013, she decided to launch Meliora. With a degree in mechanical engineering and an MBA, Mike had spent over 10 years developing new products for different companies. They married and he joined Kate in her dream of making Meliora a household brand. They started by making their products at home, turning their kitchen into a manufacturing space. They later became successful enough to have a large production facility.

3   The name *Meliora* means "better" in Latin, and Kate and Mike are proud of the ingredients they use. Many of their products contain either coconut oil or sunflower oil. They are free of plastics, dyes, and artificial fragrances; all smells come from real plants, such as lemons or peppermint. When possible, ingredients come from local providers. Kate and Mike decided at an early stage that their ingredients would not be a secret; the ingredient list is on the front of all packaging. Meliora's packaging itself is also sustainable; the company uses paper whenever possible. Surprisingly, Meliora's products are not more expensive than products made by larger companies. Kate believes better products should be affordable for all.

4   Since launching Meliora, Kate and Mike have gained a number of certifications for their products. They are a Certified B Corporation, which means they meet the highest standards of social and environmental responsibility. They are MADE SAFE certified, which means they are recognized for using non-toxic ingredients. They have been given a grade of A (on a scale of A–F) by the Environmental Working Group. They are also a Leaping Bunny company, which means Meliora's products are never tested on animals. As such, consumers can be confident the products they buy are not harming the planet.

5   In the beginning, Kate's vision was to create a business that makes positive changes. Kate and Mike have chosen a common task, household cleaning, and have created products for it that are both effective and safe. What is more, Kate and Mike are members of 1% for the Planet, a network of businesses that have promised to give 1 percent of their income to causes that make the planet a better place. Kate and Mike have also chosen to support Women's Voices for the Earth, a group that is trying to remove dangerous chemicals from our homes and communities. Providing a better way to keep our homes clean and so much more, Kate Jakubas and Mike Mayer are true social entrepreneurs.

B ANALYZE THE MODEL Work with a partner to complete an outline of the essay.

Title		
Introduction	Background	
	Thesis statement	
First body paragraph	Topic sentence	
	Supporting ideas/Details	
Second body paragraph	Topic sentence	
	Supporting ideas/Details	
Third body paragraph	Topic sentence	
	Supporting ideas/Details	
Conclusion	Final thought	

WRITING SKILL   Choose relevant information

When you are deciding what to include in an essay, think about the purpose of your essay and what information will be relevant. In other words, what do readers need to know, and what isn't important?

DO focus on answering questions that address the key points of the essay. For example, when describing a social enterprise, the reader needs to know how the business works and how it benefits society and/or the environment.

DON'T fill your essay with irrelevant details. For the same example, readers don't need to know personal information about the owners of the business unless it has a direct impact on their work.

C APPLY Reread the model essay and your outline in activity B. What other pieces of information do you think should have been included in the essay? Consider these questions and discuss your ideas with a partner.

▸ **Who** created this business? Name? Background?

▸ **What** does this business do or make? What is special about it?

▸ **When** was this business established? Where did the money come from?

▸ **Where** is this business located? Does the location influence its practices?

▸ **Why** did the owners establish this business? What motivated them?

▸ **How** have customers responded to the products or services they offer?

D NOTICE THE GRAMMAR Find the following sentences in the model and complete them. Then, with a partner, identify which verb forms are used and discuss why they are the correct choices for each sentence.

1. In establishing Meliora, these social entrepreneurs _____ a line of products that are safe for both people and the planet.

2. Meliora _____ because Kate, an environmental student, _____ interested in the ingredients used in cleaning products.

3. Kate _____ never _____ about becoming an entrepreneur, but after winning her university's Sustainable Enterprise competition in 2013, she _____ to launch Meliora.

4. Since launching Meliora, Kate and Mike _____ a number of certifications for their products.

5. Kate and Mike _____ a common task, household cleaning, and _____ products for it that are both effective and safe.

GRAMMAR   Verb forms for describing the past

Use the simple past . . .

▸ for a finished activity or sequence of events at specific times in the past.
▸ with a specific time expression in the past.

>   *First, Akhbar **wrote** a business plan. Then, he **asked** the bank for a loan.*
>   *Zita Cobb **established** the Shorefast Foundation in 2006.*

Use the past continuous . . .

▸ for an action that was already in progress when another action happened.

>   *While Ben **was traveling** in South America, he **met** many people.*

Use the present perfect . . .

▸ for an action or experience that happened at an unspecified time in the past.
▸ for something that is not yet finished, or that has a connection to the present.

>   *Zita **has created** dozens of new jobs on Fogo Island.*
>   *George **has won** several scholarships, and he plans to apply for more.*

Use the past perfect . . .

▸ for something that happened before another event or time in the past.

>   *Before Minna **went** to Japan, she **had** already **taken** a Japanese language course.*

▸ in sentences with time expressions such as *already, by the time*, and *yet*.

>   *By the time she got to Japan, she **had learned** many useful phrases.*

Note: The past perfect is not as common as the simple past. If it's clear that one action happened first, you can use the simple past.

>   *Before Minna **went** to Japan, she ~~had taken~~ **took** a Japanese course.*

E **GRAMMAR** Write the correct form of the verbs given to describe the past.

1. Amanda _____ (buy) fair trade coffee yesterday. She

   _____ (think) it _____ (taste) good.

2. While Nico _____ (study) in China, he

   _____ (take) a course in Mandarin. He

   _____ (never learn) an Asian language before.

3. When Stephanie was very young, she _____ (want) to be a

   doctor. She still does. She _____ (research) most medical

   programs in the area and knows where she wants to study.

4. Faisal _____ (want) to be an entrepreneur for a long time.

   Last week, he _____ (hire) a website designer to make a

   new website for his business.

5. The idea for my business _____ (come) to me suddenly

   when I _____ (work) for a fast-food company. I

   _____ (quit) my job and _____ (open) a

   cafe serving ethically produced snacks.

6. _____ you _____ (finish) your business

   essay yet? I _____ (submit) mine last night.

7. I _____ (not answer) the question in class this morning

   because I _____ (not read) the research.

8. Last year, our marketing team _____ (have) several

   successful campaigns, but they _____ (not do) any since.

F **EDIT** Find and correct five verb form errors.

The idea for my business started when I was traveling in Thailand. Before I

went to Thailand, I've never thought about having a business. I wanted to be a

teacher. But then I have traveled in northern Thailand, and I saw so many beautiful

items made by local craftspeople in small villages. I knew that people in my

country would love them! So first, I have talked to some community leaders.

Then I thought about ways to run a company that would help local people. I wasn't

wanting to simply make money. It was important to help others, too. Finally, I was

coming home and started a crowdfunding campaign.

PLAN & WRITE

G BRAINSTORM Work in a small group. Write a short list of businesses that want to help society and/or the environment. Choose one and use a graphic organizer like the one below to brainstorm ideas about this company and its founder(s). Here are some ideas to get you started:

product or service	owner(s)	location
date of founding	goals and strategies	success and/or reputation

Mind Map

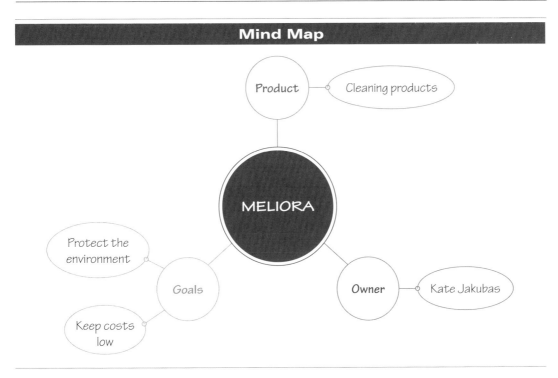

WRITING TIP

The most important sentence in an essay is the thesis statement. Everything in an essay should support it. An effective thesis statement for this writing task will tell your reader two things:

▶ Who or what your essay is about
▶ What you want to say about this organization, person, topic, or problem

While writing your first draft, check often to make sure you have not included information that is not relevant to your thesis statement.

H RESEARCH Follow the steps.

▶ Research the business you chose. Consider the questions from activity C.

▶ Decide how to organize your information. You may choose to describe the person and their business in chronological order, starting with the inspiration for the business and ending with its current status. Or you may focus on different parts of the business in each body paragraph.

I OUTLINE Complete the outline.

Introduction

Background information _____

Thesis _____

Body paragraph 1

Topic sentence _____

Supporting ideas/Details _____

Body paragraph 2

Topic sentence _____

Supporting ideas/Details _____

Body paragraph 3

Topic sentence _____

Supporting ideas/Details _____

Conclusion

Final thought _____

J FIRST DRAFT Use your outline to write a first draft of your essay. Add a title.

K REVISE Use this list as you write your second draft.

☐ Did you give basic information about your chosen business?

☐ Did you write a clear thesis statement? Does everything in your essay relate to it?

☐ Did you address different *Wh-* questions: who, what, where, when, why, how?

☐ Did you make sure to include only relevant information?

L EDIT Use this list as you write your final draft.

☐ Did you check each verb to make sure you used the correct form?

☐ Did you learn and use specialized vocabulary appropriately?

M FINAL DRAFT Reread your essay and correct any errors. Then submit it to your teacher.

REFLECT

A Check (✓) the Reflect activities you can do and the academic skills you can use.

☐ explore the role of small businesses in society

☐ collaborate on a social entrepreneurship idea

☐ consider the challenges of social entrepreneurship

☐ evaluate opportunities for social entrepreneurship

☐ write a descriptive essay about a social enterprise

☐ be an active reader

☐ choose relevant information

☐ verb forms for describing the past

☐ consider various perspectives

B Write the vocabulary words from the unit in the correct column. Add any other words that you learned. Circle words you still need to practice.

NOUN	VERB	ADJECTIVE	ADVERB & OTHER

C Reflect on the ideas in the unit as you answer these questions.

1. What is the most memorable, interesting, or helpful thing you learned in the unit?

2. Which person in the unit do you want to learn more about? Why?

3. Will you buy more products from social entrepreneurs now? Explain.

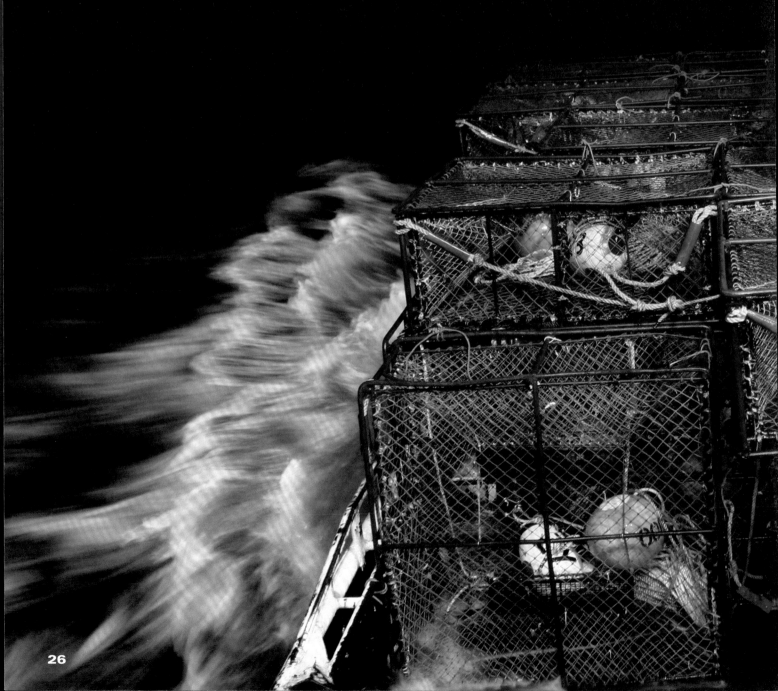

Fishing at night in the Bering Sea

IN THIS UNIT

▶ Consider the effects of caffeine consumption

▶ Relate concepts to your own experiences

▶ Evaluate the effects of electronic devices on your life

▶ Apply new information to your life

▶ Write a summary of an academic text

SKILLS

READING
Question what you read

WRITING
Summarize an academic text

GRAMMAR
Direct and indirect quotes and reporting verbs

CRITICAL THINKING
Compare research to your own experiences

CONNECT TO THE TOPIC

1. What might be some challenges of the job shown in the photo?

2. Do you ever have trouble falling asleep? What do you think causes this problem?

WATCH

CAFFEINE 101

A cafe in Florence, Italy

A Watch the first part of the video. Put the events in the correct order. ▶ 2.1

_____ The central nervous system is prevented from slowing down.

_____ The coffee drinker feels less tired and more alert.

___1___ Someone drinks a cup of coffee.

_____ The caffeine attaches itself to adenosine receptors in the brain.

_____ A compound called caffeine enters the body.

B Watch the whole video. Write T for *True* or F for *False*. ▶ 2.2

1. _____ Caffeine is found in nature.

2. _____ People only recently started to consume caffeine.

3. _____ Caffeine is consumed in different cultures around the world.

4. _____ The first tea drinkers were in Britain.

5. _____ The majority of Americans drink caffeine every day.

6. _____ You can drink up to 75 cups of coffee a day with no ill effects.

C Discuss with a partner: Do you think caffeine is potentially harmful for you? Explain.

PREPARE TO READ

A VOCABULARY Complete the sentences with the correct form of the words.

acknowledge (v)	consumption (n)	deprived (adj)	genetics (n)	stimulate (v)
adverse (adj)	contradict (v)	exhibit (v)	repetitive (adj)	uncover (v)

1. The reason why certain foods affect people in different ways has long been a mystery, but scientists are trying to _____ the truth.

2. _____ work on a machine is not only boring; it can cause problems with the muscles in your hand.

3. England is well known for its _____ of tea, but coffee is also popular there.

4. The smell of cooked food, such as freshly baked bread, _____ the appetite and makes us feel hungry.

5. I'm reading a research paper that _____ everything I have ever heard about this topic. I don't know what to believe!

6. Is obesity caused by _____, or are lifestyle choices to blame? Scientists are still exploring this question.

7. Tim suffered no _____ effects after drinking five cups of coffee during the experiment; he felt fine.

8. Three participants in the study _____ extreme signs of anxiety after drinking only two cups of coffee.

9. After hearing several criticisms, Professor Sanchez _____ that her conclusions were weak, and she needed to do further research.

10. People who are _____ of sleep often find it difficult to focus on their work.

B PERSONALIZE Discuss these questions with a partner.

1. What do you think might be one of the most **repetitive** kinds of work?
2. Have you ever had an **adverse** reaction to something you ate or drank?
3. Has your **consumption** of caffeine increased, decreased, or stayed the same in the last few years? Explain.

REFLECT Consider the effects of caffeine consumption.

You are going to read about the effects of using coffee to stay awake. Discuss these questions in a small group.

1. What are some negative effects of caffeine consumption on the human body?
2. Do you think caffeine consumption can have positive effects? If so, what?

COFFEE: MAKING THE MODERN WORLD POSSIBLE

A cafe in
New York, USA

A PREDICT Read the title and subheadings. Which point of view will the reading support? Read the article and check your prediction.

_____ Drinking coffee has serious health effects and should be avoided.

_____ For most healthy people, it's probably fine to drink a limited amount of coffee.

_____ Coffee is not as bad for you as once thought. You can drink as much as you want.

1   From Brazil to Russia, Algeria to Switzerland, people love coffee. As night-shift workers, long-distance truck drivers, or students with deadlines know, a cup of coffee can keep you awake and help you to get a job done. But is all this coffee good for you? Scientists have started to **uncover** the answer to this question—and you might be surprised by their findings.

Why do people say they need coffee?

2   Coffee contains a natural drug called caffeine, found in its leaves, seeds, and fruit. Caffeine is known to **stimulate** the brain and central nervous system, making people feel less tired. Caffeine was identified in 1820 by a German scientist, Friedlieb Ferdinand Runge. At this time, the Industrial Revolution was taking place in Europe, and factory workers, who worked long hours at **repetitive** jobs, were served coffee to prevent them from falling asleep at their machines. In this sense, caffeine has been called "the drug that made the modern world possible."

3   If caffeine was necessary in the 19th century, it is even more so today. Charles Czeisler, a researcher at Harvard University, says that for most of human existence, people's sleep cycles followed the sun; that is no longer the case. Czeisler explains, "The widespread use of caffeinated food and drink—in combination with the invention of electric light—allowed people to cope with a work schedule set by the clock, not by daylight or the natural sleep cycle." For those who have to be up when the sun is not, coffee is often a way to create and maintain a new sleep cycle.

How does caffeine work?

4   When caffeine enters the body, it reacts with a chemical called adenosine, which slows your nerve activity. It is adenosine that causes you to feel tired in the morning and after lunch. Caffeine blocks the effects of adenosine. It also increases the levels of adrenaline[1] in the blood and the brain activity of the neurotransmitters[2] dopamine and norepinephrine. The combination of these biological processes makes the coffee drinker feel more alert, often within 20 minutes of taking their first drink.

---

[1]**adrenaline** (n) a hormone that increases heart rate and improves muscular activity
[2]**neurotransmitter** (n) a chemical that sends signals to the brain

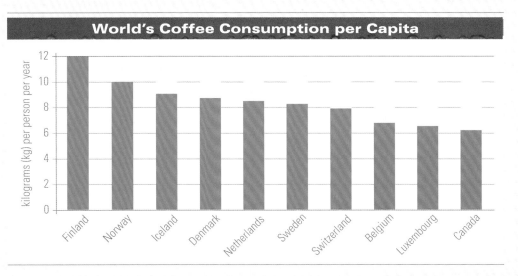

World's Coffee Consumption per Capita

kilograms (kg) per person per year

	kg per person per year
Finland	12
Norway	10
Iceland	9
Denmark	8.7
Netherlands	8.4
Sweden	8.2
Switzerland	7.9
Belgium	6.8
Luxembourg	6.5
Canada	6.2

Does everyone react to coffee in the same way?

5   No. Researchers have found that differences in **genetics** affect the way in which individuals react to coffee. Someone whose genes cause them to process caffeine more slowly might **exhibit** high blood pressure, heartburn, upset stomach, or insomnia, while someone whose body uses up caffeine quickly will experience no negative side effects.

Is drinking coffee bad for you?

6   It can be, especially if you consume multiple cups and are at risk for other health issues. Numerous studies have pointed to the **adverse** effects of caffeine; it has been connected to heart disease, digestive problems, and certain cancers, as well as to reduced sleep. It is also very addictive, and people who give up coffee report having negative side effects. However, there is new evidence that coffee is not as dangerous as once thought. Two recent studies **contradict** earlier findings. A large-scale study of over 520,000 people in 10 European countries found that coffee **consumption** was associated with *lower* risks of death from heart disease, cancer, respiratory disease, stroke, and diabetes. Similarly, a study of 185,000 participants in the United States found a connection between coffee consumption and longevity: People who drank two to four cups of coffee per day had a risk of death 18 percent lower than non-coffee drinkers. It is estimated that coffee drinkers have a 65 percent lower risk of developing Alzheimer's disease[3], a 7 percent reduced risk of diabetes, and an 84 percent lower risk of liver disease.

7   There is also some evidence that drinking coffee offers some protection against depression and other mental health concerns. In a study carried out in the United States, 50,739 women were followed over a 10-year period. Their intake of coffee, other caffeinated beverages, and decaffeinated beverages was tracked through a variety of questionnaires. Researchers concluded that the risk of depression decreased as caffeine intake increased; they admit, however, that much more research is needed.

How can the health benefits of coffee be explained?

8   Even if some research shows coffee offers these health benefits, the reason is not yet clear. Marc Gunter is an expert in cancer prevention at Imperial College London and co-author of the previously mentioned European study. He believes that the positive effects of coffee are related to the coffee bean itself. Gunter suggests, "It's something about coffee rather than something about the way that coffee is prepared or the way it's drunk." The key ingredient may not even be caffeine. German researchers Hubert Kolb, Kerstin Kempf, and Stephan Martin point out that positive health effects are also found in drinkers of decaffeinated coffee, which has about 97 percent of its caffeine removed. They propose that coffee beans share many of the same benefits as fruit and vegetables, such as broccoli and berries, and may be viewed as a "healthy vegetable food." The researchers **acknowledge**, however, that there is still more research to be done.

Does this mean I can keep drinking coffee?

9   Perhaps. These recent findings give hope to those who rely on their daily cup of coffee (or three) to get through the day. However, Charles Czeisler says, "There is a heavy, heavy price that has been paid for all this extra wakefulness." Without the recommended eight hours of sleep every night, the human body suffers physically, mentally, and emotionally. Czeisler warns, "As a society, we are tremendously sleep **deprived**." People who sleep less

---

[3]**Alzheimer's disease** (n) a disease which decreases brain functions, such as memory

than eight hours are more likely to catch colds, gain weight, or have accidents. They also have trouble focusing, make more mistakes, and are more likely to suffer from bad moods and depression.

10   The conclusion seems to be that as long as you are getting enough sleep and are generally healthy, you are probably fine to keep drinking a moderate[4] amount of coffee if you enjoy it. Harvard professor Alberto Ascherio states, "I think that the solid conclusion is that if you're a coffee drinker, keep drinking your coffee and be happy." And if you don't enjoy coffee? Ascherio says, "I think you can go on drinking your tea or water without a problem."

---

[4]**moderate** (adj) average in size or amount; neither too much nor too little

B MAIN IDEAS Which statements are true about research into coffee consumption? Choose all that apply.

_____ Researchers have uncovered the truth about the effects of coffee on the body.

_____ Some recent research contradicts earlier findings.

_____ Researchers are now in agreement that coffee is a health food.

_____ More research into the effects of coffee on the body is needed.

C DETAILS Check the *incorrect* piece of information.

1. Caffeine . . .

   _____ stimulates the central nervous system.

   _____ was invented in 1820.

   _____ helps people to stay awake.

2. People rely on coffee today because . . .

   _____ they work harder than in the past.

   _____ their work schedules are not set by the sun.

   _____ they may need to work when they have not slept enough.

3. Caffeine . . .

   _____ can affect a person within 20 minutes.

   _____ affects different people in different ways.

   _____ always causes high blood pressure.

4. Drinking too much coffee has been associated with increased risk for . . .

   _____ diabetes.

   _____ cancer.

   _____ heart disease.

5. Recent studies have indicated that . . .

   _____ coffee may not be as dangerous as once thought.

   _____ drinking decaffeinated coffee does not have the same benefits as regular coffee.

   _____ coffee may offer some protection against disease.

6. We can conclude that . . .

   _____ more research into coffee drinking is needed.

   _____ we can safely drink as much coffee as we want.

   _____ occasional coffee drinking is probably not dangerous.

> **LEARNING TIP**
>
> Do you rely on coffee to get you through a long night of studying? A more effective approach is to become aware of your own study preferences and work with them. A study of 48 university students in the U.K. found that 37 percent were "early birds" who preferred to work in the morning, 41 percent were "night owls" who liked to work at night, and the rest were happy to study at any time. Try to identify your own personal body clock, and plan your study schedule to match it.

D DETAILS Who said it? Match each person to the correct statement.

1. _____ Charles Czeisler

2. _____ Marc Gunter

3. _____ Hubert Kolb, Kerstin Kempf, and Stephan Martin

4. _____ Alberto Ascherio

a. "I think that the solid conclusion is that if you're a coffee drinker, keep drinking your coffee and be happy."

b. Coffee may be viewed as a "healthy vegetable food."

c. "There is a heavy, heavy price that has been paid for all this extra wakefulness."

d. "It's something about coffee rather than something about the way that coffee is prepared or the way it's drunk."

READING SKILL Question what you read

As you carry out research, remember that you cannot trust everything you read. Here are some questions to ask when looking at research findings:

▶ Where was this information published? Has it been evaluated by other experts in the field?

▶ Who is responsible for this study? What are the researchers' credentials? Are they qualified to carry out this research?

▶ How long ago was the experiment carried out? Is it still valid today?

▶ How many participants were involved in the study? Is this number enough to make valid conclusions?

▶ What method was used to obtain the results? Was the methodology appropriate?

▶ Would the same results be found if a different researcher carried out the same study with a different group of participants or in a different part of the world?

E APPLY You are doing research for an essay about sleep and young people, and you find the information below. What question(s) would you ask about the findings? Discuss your thoughts with a partner.

▶ An article argues that a certain medicine can offset the negative effects of sleep deprivation. You learn that the research was funded by a company that produces this drug.

▶ An article outlines the adverse health effects experienced by college students who consumed popular energy drinks. This research was published in 1999.

▶ An article states that students who described themselves as "happy" or "very happy" reported better sleep habits than those who described themselves as "unhappy."

▶ A magazine article reports on an experiment that found most young people in a specific country sleep at least eight hours per night and are not sleep deprived.

REFLECT Relate concepts to your own experiences.

Consider the main points of the reading *Coffee: Making the Modern World Possible* and discuss these questions in a small group.

1. Caffeine has been called "the drug that made the modern world possible." Do you agree? Explain.

2. If you had to give a recommendation about drinking coffee, what would it be? In what way(s) would your recommendation change depending on who you were talking to?

3. Has the passage made you think about your own coffee consumption? Are you going to do anything different? Explain.

PREPARE TO READ

A VOCABULARY Choose the sentence that shows the meaning of the word in bold.

1. Leo is always complaining about his **ailments**. He should see a doctor.

    a. He has frequent illnesses.   b. He has a lot of accidents.

2. The two countries have a history of conflict, but now they are **aligned** on many issues.

    a. The countries agree.   b. The countries disagree.

3. Jill has **chronic** stomach pains; she feels unwell whenever she is stressed.

    a. She rarely experiences pain.   b. Her pains are a long-term problem.

4. If you have poor vision at night, you might have a **deficiency** in vitamin A.

    a. You have a lack of vitamin A.   b. You have too much vitamin A.

5. My friend's phone calls are a **disturbance** to my study routine.

    a. The calls are a welcome break.   b. The calls make it difficult for me to study.

6. I set up my email to **filter out** messages from mailing lists. That way I get less junk mail.

    a. It removes the messages.   b. It makes the messages bigger.

7. Her financial situation was an **impediment** to her goal.

    a. Her goal was made more difficult.   b. Her goal was made easier.

8. Stress can often **interfere with** your performance on an exam.

    a. It can be helpful.   b. It can cause problems.

9. Eating chicken soup helps to **mitigate** the effects of a cold.

    a. It improves your condition.   b. It makes your condition worse.

10. Drinking water is known to **suppress** hunger.

    a. It increases hunger.   b. It reduces hunger.

B PERSONALIZE Discuss these questions with a partner.

1. What kinds of diets can cause a **deficiency** of important nutrients in the body?

2. What, in your experience, **interferes** with the quality of your sleep?

3. Can you see any **impediments** to your goals? Explain.

REFLECT   Evaluate the effects of electronic devices on your life.

You are going to read about the effects of technology on sleep. Discuss these questions in a small group.

1. What advantages have electronic devices brought to your life? Have they brought any disadvantages?

2. What devices could you not live without? Why?

3. Do you find it easy or difficult to fall asleep after using your electronic devices?

TECHNOLOGY AND SLEEP: WHAT IS THE CONNECTION?

The Japanese term *inemuri* means "sleeping while present" and occurs when a person sleeps in a place not meant for sleep, such as this subway station in Tokyo.

A PREVIEW Answer the questions.

1. In what ways might devices such as laptops, tablets, and mobile phones keep you awake?

2. In what ways might these devices help you to sleep?

2.2 *If you cannot sleep at night, the problem might be the amount of coffee you have consumed during the day. The amount of screen time you enjoy before bed might also be to blame . . .*

1   Do you find it hard to fall asleep at night? Your computer—or even your phone—may be to blame. When we use devices late at night, whether to work, chat, or play games, our internal clocks get confused: Is it daytime or night time? Should we be awake or asleep? Frequent users of technology are often advised to turn off their devices an hour or two before bed and to spend that time taking a calming bath or doing exercise. This, however, may not always be realistic for students with deadlines, or even for people who enjoy watching videos as a way to relax after a long day. How does the use of electronic devices affect the brain and keep us awake? And is there any way these devices could be used differently to help us sleep?

2   The human body, like that of other animals, insects, and even plants, has a natural 24-hour biological cycle, known as the circadian rhythm. In the past, when people's waking and sleeping hours followed the rising and setting of the sun, our circadian rhythms were **aligned** with nature. This is not the case today. We are constantly exposed to light from artificial sources, including electronic devices. This causes **disturbances** to our circadian rhythms, with possibly serious effects for our health.

3   The human circadian rhythm is controlled by a hormone[1] called melatonin, produced in the pineal gland in the brain. When it gets dark, our bodies naturally produce melatonin, which makes us feel sleepy; for this reason, melatonin is sometimes called the "sleep hormone." In short, melatonin tells us when it's time for bed. In the daytime, less melatonin is produced; this tells us to stay awake. People who travel across several time

---

[1]**hormone** (n) a chemical in the body that helps to control the function of organs

Light's Effect on Melatonin Production

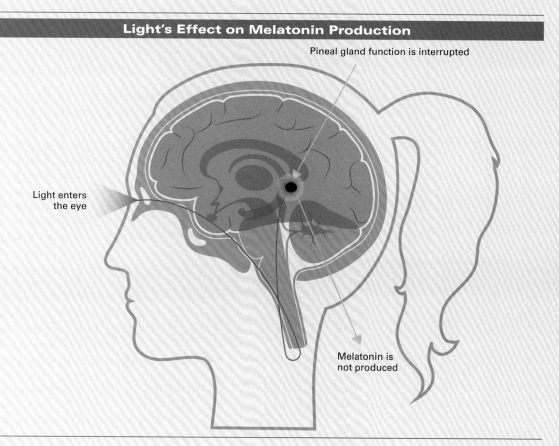

Pineal gland function is interrupted

Light enters the eye

Melatonin is not produced

Computers and phones produce a blue light that interrupts our natural sleep cycle.

zones and who are unable to sleep at night are sometimes advised to take melatonin pills to **mitigate** the effects of jet lag.

4   What does this have to do with your electronic devices? Devices such as computers and phones produce a blue light. This blue light **suppresses** the production of melatonin. If you find it hard to fall asleep after watching a late-night video on your laptop, it could be because your melatonin levels are low. Melatonin **deficiency** can lead to insomnia: You are unable to fall asleep, since your body has received messages to the contrary. This disruption to our circadian rhythm has been associated with a variety of **ailments**, including **chronic** digestive problems, lower energy levels, and depression.

5   However, recent research has suggested that the effects of blue light on the brain, and consequently, on our sleep quality, are not fully understood. A 2019 study at the University of Manchester, U.K., indicates that yellow light might actually **interfere with** sleep more than blue light. Researchers suggest that yellow light might trick the body into thinking it is daylight, whereas blue light might tell the body that it's evening. It is important to keep in mind that sleep research is often carried out with mice, which are nocturnal[2] animals, and they may not react in the same way as humans. Clearly, biologists do not yet have all the answers.

6   Despite the lack of agreement about blue light, there are other important ways in which your devices might keep you awake. First, the use of devices delays the onset of REM sleep, the period of sleep in which you dream. This is problematic, as insufficient REM sleep is associated with anxiety, depression, and an inability to concentrate. Second, using devices keeps your brain active. When you've enjoyed a chat with a friend, a movie, or a game, it can be hard to relax; you want to keep thinking about what you've watched or talked about. Finally, if you keep your phone near your bed, you risk being woken up by various beeps and pings when you receive a text or email.

7   It seems clear, then, that the use of technology can be a serious **impediment** to a good night's sleep and that it is best avoided before bed. But is this absolutely necessary? Recent developments in technology have made it possible for devices to actually help give you a *better* night's sleep. Many devices now have a setting that allows the user to **filter out** blue light. Three other possibly beneficial effects of using devices at night are as follows:

[2]**nocturnal** (adj) awake and active at night; asleep during the day

▶ **White noise.** White noise is peaceful background noise, such as the sound of ocean waves or a light rainfall. If you live in a city and are kept awake by the noise of traffic or people shouting outside your window, a white noise app might be a good investment.

▶ **Nighttime exercises.** There are various apps that can help you to relax before sleep by leading you through a series of breathing or meditation exercises. Users of these apps report feeling less stressed and able to drift off into a peaceful sleep.

▶ **Awareness-raising devices.** You may know that fitness trackers can alert you when you have walked 10,000 steps each day. Newer versions of these devices can help you track not only how many hours of sleep you get each night, but also the quality of your sleep. Users can review their sleep data and then take actions to improve their sleep or keep doing what is working.

8   So, should you remove all of your devices from your bedroom if you want to get a good night's sleep? Not necessarily—but be aware of the biological effects of artificial light, and think carefully about how and why you are using these devices late at night.

B MAIN IDEAS Answer the questions.

1. What is the main idea of this reading?

    a. People who cannot sleep should adjust the filters on their devices.

    b. We sleep better when we follow our natural circadian rhythms.

    c. Manufacturers of electronic devices need to learn more about the biology of sleep.

    d. The effects of using technology before sleep are complex.

2. What is the first thing we should do if we want to have a good night's sleep?

    a. Understand the effects of technology on the brain.

    b. Remove all electronic gadgets from the bedroom.

    c. Avoid yellow light when we are trying to sleep.

    d. Buy an app that helps us track our sleep.

C DETAILS Which choice best expresses the meaning of these sentences from the reading?

1. *People who travel across several time zones and who are unable to sleep at night are sometimes advised to take melatonin pills to mitigate the effects of jet lag.* (par. 3)

    a. When you travel overnight, taking melatonin pills will make your jet lag worse.

    b. Melatonin makes you sleepy, and it is best not to travel overnight.

    c. Melatonin pills can help overnight travelers fall asleep at the right time.

2. *It is important to keep in mind that sleep research is often carried out with mice, which are nocturnal animals, and they may not react in the same way as humans.* (par. 5)

    a. Mice may be more sensitive to light than humans.

    b. Research results found in mice may not be the same as those found in humans.

    c. Nocturnal animals, such as mice, can tell us a lot about the function of the brain.

3. *This is problematic, as insufficient REM sleep is associated with anxiety, depression, and an inability to concentrate.* (par. 6)

    a. REM sleep is important; we need to dream to keep good mental health.

    b. Dreaming during REM sleep is beneficial because it keeps our brains active.

    c. It is good to delay the onset of REM sleep whenever possible.

CRITICAL THINKING Compare research to your own experiences

When you conduct research, you may come across contradictory evidence. Who are you going to trust? Think about the questions from this unit's Reading Skill box, but also remember that you are a key player in this process. Even if a study seems believable, consider (a) other things you have read and (b) your own experiences. Just because something is printed on paper or appears on the Internet, it is not necessarily true for every person and in every context. Trust yourself to recognize when more information is needed and you need to investigate more.

D APPLY For each statement, check Yes for *I have experienced this* or No for *I have not experienced this.* Then survey your classmates. How do your responses and those of your classmates support or contradict the reading passages in this unit?

	YOU		CLASSMATES	
	Yes	**No**	**Yes**	**No**
1. Many people experience heartburn, upset stomach, or insomnia after drinking coffee or tea.				
2. People who are sleep deprived are more likely to catch colds, gain weight, or have accidents.				
3. When we use electronic devices in bed, our brains get the message that sleep should be avoided.				
4. When our circadian rhythms are disrupted, we experience lower energy levels and depression.				
5. When we've enjoyed a chat with a friend online, it can be hard to relax and drift into sleep.				
6. Breathing and meditation apps can help people to fall asleep.				

REFLECT   Apply new information to your life.

Discuss these questions in a small group. Take notes in your notebook.

1. Has this article made you think about your own use of technology before bed? Are you going to do anything different? Explain.

2. Have you ever tried an app to help you relax and fall asleep? If not, are you interested in trying one now?

3. How would you respond to someone who said, "I think the focus on circadian rhythms is exaggerated. Humans have learned to adapt to modern society."?

WRITE

Write a summary of an academic text.

You are going to write a summary of the reading *Technology and Sleep: What Is the Connection?* Use the ideas, vocabulary, and skills from the unit.

A PREPARE When you read academic material, you will often need to summarize information into a short paragraph. You will need to decide what to include and what to leave out. Read the text and highlight key information.

Cognitive Effects of Sleep Deprivation in University Students
Patrick, Y., Lee, A., Raha, O. *et. al.* **(2017)**

Sleep deprivation is common among university students who live in a culture that, due to work and active social lives, promotes little sleep. Other reasons for poor sleep include caffeine intake and technology, which prevent students from getting sufficient sleep. While many studies have investigated the effects of sleep deprivation, few have focused on university students. However, students say that sleep problems have a huge impact on their academic performance. This study aimed to determine whether a night of sleep deprivation, equivalent to an "all-nighter," would have a negative impact on the cognitive performance of students. It focused specifically on working memory, cognitive function, and reaction time.

This study took place from June to September 2015. The study sample consisted of 64 students at Imperial College London; 57 students (89 percent) completed the study. Of the participants, 58 percent were male and 42 percent were female. The participants' average age was 22 years. Participants were recruited directly or through posters on campus, social media, and a newsletter. Participants' travel expenses were reimbursed, and all participants were offered the opportunity to enter a raffle. Participants were told that the study was related to sleep deprivation, but were not told the expected results. All participants gave written consent to participate. The study was approved by the Medical Education Ethics Committee, Imperial College London.

Participants were randomly divided into two groups: One would have a normal night's sleep, and the other would be deprived of sleep. Twenty-four hours before the morning assessment, participants were told to avoid caffeinated drinks. Those having a normal night's sleep were asked to report how much they had slept. Those in the sleep deprivation group were required to fill out a form every 45 minutes to confirm that they were still awake. This form was checked the following morning.

Participants' memory was then tested by showing them a sequence of colors and sounds and asking them to repeat what they saw and heard. As each level progressed, another color-sound combination was added to the previous sequence. This test was repeated three times.

Cognitive processing was tested by using the Stroop test: Participants see a mismatch between the name of a color and the ink with which this color is written (for example, the word *green* is written in purple ink). They are then asked to name only the color of the ink.

Reaction speed was tested using the ruler drop test. The researcher held a ruler vertically and let it drop without warning. The participants had to catch the ruler as it fell. They were allowed to practice three times. Statistical analysis was carried out on these tests.

Results showed that negative cognitive effects were not as widespread as previously thought. A comparison of test results revealed no significant difference on the memory test, with essential components of memory being maintained for both sleep deprivation and normal sleep groups. There was also no significant difference between the two groups on the Stroop test. There was a slight difference on the reaction test, with the sleep-deprived group demonstrating slower reaction times.

This study indicates that one night of sleep deprivation has minimal effect on a student's cognitive capacity. Results suggest that the young student population may be more effective at dealing with minor sleep deprivation than their older counterparts. Overall, this study found that the occasional "all-nighter" does not significantly affect a student's cognitive ability.

Several limitations need to be considered when interpreting the findings of this study. First, participants carried out their night of sleep deprivation in an environment of their choice, rather than a supervised environment. Further, the study design relied on participants self-reporting their sleep deprivation effects on a form.

B MODEL Read the summary of the study in activity A. Compare the information with what you highlighted.

Summary of Sleep Deprivation Study

Patrick et al. (2017) investigated the effect of a sleepless night on the memory, cognitive functioning, and reaction times of 57 university students in London. Participants were divided into two groups: one with a full night's sleep and one that was sleep deprived. They were asked to repeat sequences of colors and sounds, take a Stroop test, and catch a dropped ruler. The researchers reported that the sleep-deprived participants demonstrated fewer cognitive difficulties than anticipated, with differences only on the reaction test. This suggests that university students can have an occasional "all-nighter" with minimal negative cognitive effects.

C ANALYZE THE MODEL Review the summary of the study in activity B. Add notes to the chart. If no information is given, write *NI*.

	Information	What does the summary say?
1.	Purpose of the study	*To investigate the effect of a sleepless night on the memory, cognitive functioning, and reaction times of university students*
2.	Number of participants	
3.	How the participants were selected	
4.	What reward they were given	
5.	Ethical considerations of the study	
6.	What the participants had to do	
7.	Explanations of the Stroop and ruler tests	
8.	Results of the study	
9.	Significance of the findings	
10.	Limitations of the study	

WRITING SKILL   Summarize an academic text

When you write a summary, follow these steps:

1. Read the material carefully. Make sure you understand it.

2. Highlight (or take notes on) the key points. In a research study, these will be (a) the problem under investigation; (b) what research has shown about the problem; and (c) what conclusions can be drawn from this research.

3. Write the first draft of your summary. Focus on covering the main points. Remember to paraphrase information.

4. Revise your summary. Make sure you have included all the main points and that you have not included unnecessary details or repetition.

5. Check that your summary will make sense to someone who has not read the original. A reader should get the main points from only reading your summary.

6. Check and correct grammar, spelling, and punctuation.

D NOTICE THE GRAMMAR Find the following sentences in *Coffee: Making the Modern World Possible*. Complete the sentences with the missing verbs. With a partner, discuss why the author uses these verbs instead of repeating the verb *say*.

1. Czeisler _____, "The widespread use of caffeinated food and drink—in combination with the invention of electric light—allowed people to cope with a work schedule set by the clock, not by daylight or the natural sleep cycle." (par. 3)

2. Gunter _____, "It's something about coffee rather than something about the way that coffee is prepared or the way it's drunk." (par. 8)

3. Hubert Kolb, Kerstin Kempf, and Stephan Martin _____ that positive health effects are also found in drinkers of decaffeinated coffee, which has about 97 percent of its caffeine removed. (par. 8)

4. Czeisler _____, "As a society, we are tremendously sleep deprived." (par. 9)

GRAMMAR   Direct and indirect quotes and reporting verbs

When reporting what an author has written, you can use the writer's exact words with quotation marks, or you can paraphrase. Direct quotes are best when the writer expresses an idea in particularly strong or effective words. Quoting indirectly with your own words (paraphrasing) is a good way to summarize the main idea of long quotes. In either case, use a reporting verb.

> **Direct quote:** Garcia *argues*, "After our extensive study, we determined sleep is undoubtedly the most important factor in student success."

> **Indirect quote:** Garcia *argues* that sleep is crucial to student success.

Note that in reporting research, you should use the present unless the research was carried out a long time ago.

Common **reporting verbs** are *say* and *state*. Other reporting verbs include *argue, conclude, point out, explain, insist, suggest, add,* and *propose*. Reporting verbs carry different weights in meaning. For example, *say* is neutral, whereas *argue* or *insist* are more forceful.

Another way to report what an author has written is to use the phrase "According to . . ." When you choose this option, you do not need to add "he/she says . . .":

> ✓ *According to Jones, technology at night does more harm than good.*

> ✗ *According to Jones, she says technology at night does more harm than good.*

E GRAMMAR Look at the verbs below. Do they generally indicate a stronger, neutral, or softer argument for a point? Write each verb where you think it belongs on the line below. Then compare your answers with a partner.

add	conclude	insist	propose	state
argue	explain	point out	say	suggest

←——→

Stronger   **Neutral**   **Softer**

F GRAMMAR Rewrite the statements using indirect quotes and your own words. Choose a suitable verb. There is more than one correct answer.

1. Anderson and May: "The results show that online white noise applications are helpful in reducing insomnia for people living in urban areas."

   _____

   _____

2. Nguyen: "There is no doubt whatsoever that energy drinks should not be consumed by young people under the age of 18."

   _____

   _____

3. Dunn, Collins, and Wilson: "Schools could perhaps offer workshops to high school students to teach them about the dangers of using technology late at night."

   _____

   _____

4. McDonald: "Melatonin pills are helpful for people with jet lag because they trick the body into staying awake and falling asleep at the right time."

   _____

   _____

5. Molina and Chen: "Another problem is that people are woken up by text messages and emails."

   _____

   _____

G EDIT Read the paragraph. Find and correct four errors.

If you are trying to limit the amount of coffee you drink before bed, there are other warm drinks you might enjoy. One of the best drinks in the evening is chamomile tea. As Ivanova explains, This tea is made of dried chamomile flowers and has several health benefits." Scott (2020) suggested that chamomile is beneficial for stomach problems, a view supported by Watson (2020). According to Jenkins, she concludes that chamomile is the best tea for people with insomnia. However, Wang (2021) is warning that chamomile should not be consumed by people who have allergies to plants.

PLAN & WRITE

H Review the reading *Technology and Sleep: What Is the Connection?*. Highlight the key details that should be included in a summary. Then discuss your choices in a small group.

I OUTLINE Use the outline to plan your summary.

Opening sentence (What is the main idea that you want to express in your summary?)

_____

_____

Key points

What problem is identified here? _____

_____

What has research shown us about this issue? _____

_____

_____

What is one conclusion from the research? _____

_____

_____

What is a different conclusion from other research?

_____

_____

Concluding sentence (What can we learn from research into technology and sleep?)

_____

_____

J FIRST DRAFT With the Writing Skill steps in mind, write a first draft of your summary from your highlighted information. Make sure to paraphrase and use reporting verbs. Avoid copying sentences word for word unless you are including one very important quotation.

K REVISE Use this list as you write your second draft.

- ☐ Did you introduce the main idea of your summary in your first sentence?
- ☐ Did you identify the problem being investigated?
- ☐ Did you include information about different research on the topic?
- ☐ Did you cover all the main ideas?
- ☐ Did you use your own words?
- ☐ Did you avoid any information that doesn't belong in a short summary?
- ☐ Did you include a concluding sentence?

L EDIT Use this list as you write your final draft.

- ☐ Did you spell names and technical terms correctly?
- ☐ Did you use a variety of reporting verbs? Are they appropriate?
- ☐ Did you use "According to . . ." correctly?
- ☐ Did you use the correct verb form for each situation?
- ☐ Did you use appropriate synonyms and/or different wording when paraphrasing?

M FINAL DRAFT Reread your summary, clarify any unclear ideas, and correct any errors. Then submit it to your teacher.

A camper using an electronic device

REFLECT

A Check (✓) the Reflect activities you can do and the academic skills you can use.

☐ consider the effects of caffeine consumption

☐ relate concepts to your own experiences

☐ evaluate the effects of electronic devices on your life

☐ apply new information to your life

☐ write a summary of an academic text

☐ question what you read

☐ summarize an academic text

☐ direct and indirect quotes and reporting verbs

☐ compare research to your own experiences

B Write the vocabulary words from the unit in the correct column. Add any other words that you learned. Circle words you still need to practice.

NOUN	VERB	ADJECTIVE	ADVERB & OTHER

C Reflect on the ideas in the unit as you answer these questions.

1. What was the most memorable, interesting, or helpful thing you learned in the unit?

_____

_____

2. How has the unit made you evaluate your own use of coffee, tea, and/or electronic devices before bed? Will you think differently about using these things in the future?

_____

_____

3. What will you do in the future to ensure you get a good night's sleep?

_____

_____

WORKING TOGETHER

The Qian Jin acrobatic troupe practice in Shenyang, China.

IN THIS UNIT

- ▶ Consider what makes a team successful
- ▶ Carry out a SWOT analysis for a team
- ▶ Generate strategies for successful teamwork
- ▶ Design a plan that requires teamwork
- ▶ Write an expository essay on teamwork

SKILLS

READING
Determine a writer's purpose and audience

WRITING
Paraphrase research material

GRAMMAR
Modals and expressions for advice

CRITICAL THINKING
Recognize a writer's cultural context

CONNECT TO THE TOPIC

1. What do you think is needed for these acrobats to work so well together?
2. Have you ever been part of a team? How well did your team work together?

TEAM-BUILDING: THE MARSHMALLOW CHALLENGE

A Watch the video. Complete the sentences to show how the challenge works. ▶ 3.1

1. The goal of the challenge is to build the _____ freestanding structure.

2. Teams have _____ minutes to complete the challenge.

3. Team members need:

   a. _____ pieces of dry spaghetti

   b. One meter of _____ and one meter of _____

   c. One pair of _____

   d. One large _____

B Watch again. What can people learn from this challenge? ▶ 3.1

_____

_____

C If you could try the marshmallow challenge, what might your structure look like? Draw your design idea and discuss it with a partner.

PREPARE TO READ

A VOCABULARY Complete the sentences with the correct words.

competence (n)	discriminate (v)	friction (n)	outcome (n)	skeptical (adj)
comprehensive (adj)	elite (adj)	insight (n)	reluctant (adj)	unity (n)

1. Barbara is _____ to go camping. She is anxious about wild animals.

2. In times of crisis, national _____ is important. Everyone needs to work together to get through difficult times.

3. Professor Holding has written a _____ guide to successful communication in the workplace. It covers everything an employee needs to know.

4. What was the _____ of the meeting? Were any important decisions made?

5. Her biography provided _____ into how she became successful at such a young age.

6. There was some _____ between Kate and Markus when they started working together, but now that they know each other better, they get along quite well.

7. The world's _____ athletes compete in the Olympic Games every four years.

8. In many countries today, it is illegal for employers to _____ against people with disabilities; everyone must be treated equally.

9. The manager is confident that the project will be finished by the end of the year. Most employees, however, are _____ and think it will take longer.

10. Dave was included on the team because of his _____ in computer programming. On top of that, he is easy to work with.

B PERSONALIZE Discuss these questions with a partner.

1. When have you been **skeptical** about a plan? Were you right to be skeptical?

2. Think of a competition, in sports or in another activity, that you have taken part in. What was the **outcome**?

3. If you were asked to be a team leader, would you be excited about the opportunity, or would you be **reluctant** to take on the responsibility? Explain.

REFLECT Consider what makes a team successful.

You are going to read about teamwork in sports. Discuss these questions in a small group.

1. What qualities do you think a sports team needs to be successful?

2. If a team is not doing well, what might be the reasons?

3. How do you define success in a sports team? Besides winning games, what else can be gained from playing?

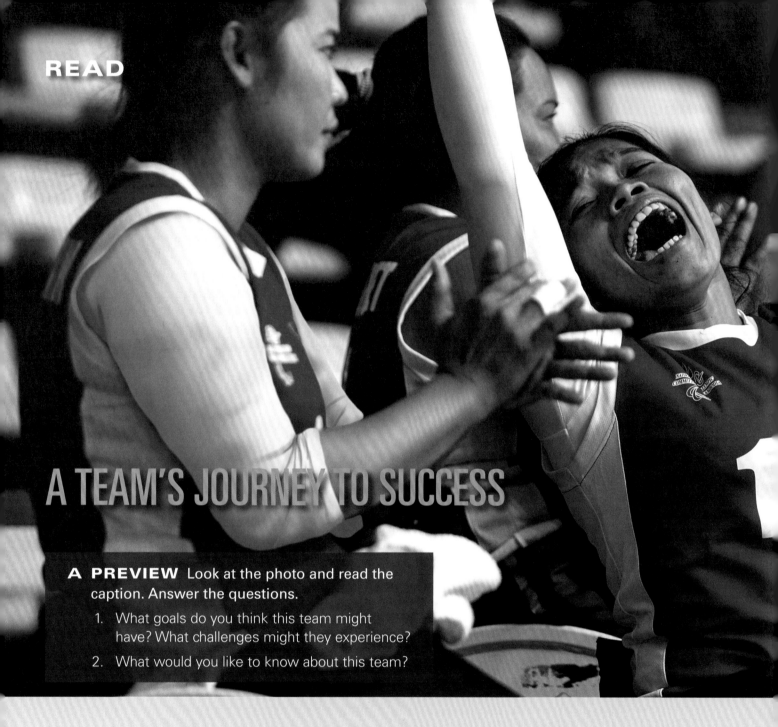

A TEAM'S JOURNEY TO SUCCESS

A PREVIEW Look at the photo and read the caption. Answer the questions.

1. What goals do you think this team might have? What challenges might they experience?

2. What would you like to know about this team?

🎧 3.1

1   In Battambang, Cambodia, Sieng Sokchan was training for the experience of her life. Sieng was the captain and coach of a basketball team for women with disabilities, and she had recently learned that she would be leading the Cambodian national team to their first international competition. She was going to the 2018 Asian Para Games in Jakarta, Indonesia, where she would join 3,000 athletes from 43 countries in a celebration of sports for competitors with disabilities. Of the 12 members of Sieng's team, 7 had been selected from her own team, the Battambang Roses. For Sieng, who acquired her

disability as a child and had since made sports her passion, the trip to Indonesia was a dream come true.

2   When Sieng was a child, street fights were quite common in her town. One day when she was 11, Sieng was helping at her grandmother's market stall. She felt a strange sensation in her back. She had been shot by a stray bullet. Although she was rushed to the hospital, Sieng did not have an x-ray until a week later, and by that time, it was too late. Her spine had been damaged, and she would never walk again.

3   Looking back on the years following the accident, Sieng remembers, "Dark thoughts often lingered[1] in my head. I felt angry, but there was

Members of Cambodia's national women's basketball team cheer at the 2018 Asian Para Games in Jakarta, Indonesia.

no one to talk to." That all changed one day when she was introduced to wheelchair basketball by the International Committee of the Red Cross (ICRC). She immediately fell in love with the game, and when she scored her first basket, she felt a sense of achievement she had never experienced before. Sieng was then asked to form a basketball team for women with disabilities. She was **skeptical** at first, but she accepted the challenge, and her team, the Battambang Roses, was born. Now, after years of training and winning local competitions, Sieng and her team members were going to Indonesia to compete internationally. As captain, Sieng would have a critical role to play in leading her team.

4   Psychologists look for **insights** into how groups of individuals come together to accomplish a goal, and what makes a team successful. One of the best-known models for teamwork was proposed by Bruce Tuckman, who names five stages which teams— athletic, professional, or recreational—usually pass through on their way to success. Tuckman's five stages can be seen in Sieng's journey to the Asian Para Games.

---

[1]**linger** (v) to stay for a long time

5 **Forming** This is when the team comes together. Members are chosen for both their **competence** and their personal characteristics. At this stage, there is a sense of excitement about being on the team, but also anxiety about the **outcome**. Sieng remembers, "It was hard to look for women to play this sport. First, they didn't know how to operate the wheelchairs or how to dribble[2] the ball and shoot the ball, so they were **reluctant** to take part in the beginning." The women she approached had not only never played basketball before, they were also dealing with poverty and a lack of medical resources. Sieng achieved success in this stage by promising friendship, emotional support, and increased fitness to the women she persuaded to join.

6 **Storming** This is the most stressful step in the team's progress. Problems within the team might emerge as team members get used to working together. Sieng admits that sometimes there were fights or jealousy as the players worked to establish their own roles within the team. However, as a woman with a disability, she told her team, "Our society is already **discriminating** against us. We must be kind to each other. If we don't love and support each other first, no one will." By showing understanding and compassion toward each individual player, Sieng brought her team together.

7 **Norming** By now, team members are working well together, overcoming challenges, and making progress. The Battambang Roses took part in a **comprehensive** training program, so they could raise the level of their game and compete against others. Sieng remembers, "Training women to this level of the game hasn't been easy. We all have different struggles and had to work harder than everyone to overcome them." But every time they saw the ball go through the hoop, the women realized how strong their bodies were. This kept them motivated. As the team made progress, they started to play at the national and international levels, winning games against teams from India, South Korea, and Laos.

8 **Performing** Preparation has paid off, and the team is now working well together with minimal **friction**. The team's objectives are within sight. As it turned out, the Cambodian team did not win a medal at the Asian Para Games in Jakarta. In fact, playing against **elite** teams such as China and Thailand, they lost all their games and finished in last place. But their performance was not a failure. Playing in their first major international competition, they won something more important: recognition, for their own achievements and for all women with disabilities in the sports community. Sieng says, "I still think we are winners."

9 **Mourning**[3] Tuckman added this fifth step at a later stage in his research. At this stage, the team's work is done, and the team members may go their separate ways. This is often a time of mixed feelings. If the team's objectives have been met, this may be a time of celebration. If the team has not succeeded, there may be feelings of regret and frustration. Even if the team has worked well, there may still be feelings of sadness if the team members have formed a close connection and may not work together again. Fortunately for Sieng, her journey with her team was not over. She would continue to play a game she loved, with a group of women she now called sisters.

10 Looking back on her journey to Indonesia, Sieng has no regrets. For these women, team membership has led to a transformation in their lives, bringing achievement, confidence, and belief in themselves. Perhaps most importantly, it brought a sense of **unity**. As Sieng says, "The important thing is for the team to trust and believe in each other. We love each other because we are on the same team."

---

[2]**dribble** (v) to move a basketball by bouncing it along the ground

[3]**mourn** (v) to feel sadness after the death or end of something

Members of the Battambang Roses practice in Cambodia.

B MAIN IDEAS Match each stage of Tuckman's framework with the correct statement.

1. _____ Forming

2. _____ Storming

3. _____ Norming

4. _____ Performing

5. _____ Mourning

a. "I don't know why the others won't see my point of view. I know my ideas are the best. Why won't they listen to me?"

b. "We've really achieved something. We're all proud of what we've done, but we'll miss each other."

c. "We're really doing well! I'm feeling good about everything we've accomplished so far.

d. "I'm excited to be on the team, but I'm nervous, too. What if we don't achieve our goals?"

e. "We've dealt with our differences of opinion, and we've established a routine. We're starting to see results."

C DETAILS Find and correct eight errors in the summary of Sieng Sokchan's journey.

Sieng Sokchan started playing wheelchair basketball as a young girl, after she was injured in a car accident. When she first learned to play basketball, she hated the game. Sieng agreed to establish a team especially for women with disabilities. She called her team the Battambang Roses, after the town where she lived. Sieng found it difficult to attract players since many women were dealing with poverty and a lack of medical resources. However, she promised them friendship and financial support, and the team came together. The team members never had disagreements or experienced jealousy of each other. They learned to work together well, and after a short training program, they started to play against other teams. Eventually, Sieng was asked to lead the Cambodian national team in a competition in Japan. Seven members of the national team were from Sieng's own team in Battambang. At the competition, they played against weaker teams, such as China and Thailand, and finished in first place. Sieng is proud of her team, as they have shown the power of women with disabilities.

READING SKILL Determine a writer's purpose and audience

From books to messages on social media, all writing has a specific **purpose**. The writer wants the reader to react in a certain way. Some purposes are:

- ▶ to inform/educate
- ▶ to advise
- ▶ to entertain

- ▶ to persuade
- ▶ to warn
- ▶ to sell

Every piece of writing also has an intended **audience**, and this influences how writers write. If the audience is familiar with a topic, the author will not explain basic information. If the audience is unfamiliar with a topic, the text will be written to reflect that.

As you are reading, ask yourself these questions:

- ▶ Why did the author write this? If you know, for example, that the goal is to sell something, you may respond to it more critically than you would if the goal were to entertain.
- ▶ Who was the author writing for? If you are looking for detailed academic material, you will not find articles written for a general audience very helpful.

D APPLY Review the reading and discuss these questions in a small group.

1. Why did the author tell the story of the Cambodian wheelchair basketball team? How do you think the author wanted the reader to react? How did *you* react to this story?

2. How might this story be changed if the audience were (a) people who have never heard about sports for people with disabilities; or (b) people deciding whether or not to donate to sports programs for people with disabilities?

E APPLY Work with a partner to complete the table.

Text	Purpose	Audience
A 350-page history of Real Madrid soccer team	*to entertain readers*	
An advertisement for a workshop on team-building skills		
A blog post about how to deal with difficult colleagues		
An essay written by a student in a psychology course		
A journal article sharing research about teams		

REFLECT Carry out a SWOT analysis for a team.

In a SWOT analysis, you evaluate the Strengths, Weaknesses, Opportunities, and Threats of an idea or organization. Think about a team you have been part of. Write answers to these questions in your notebook and discuss with a partner. Then share your thoughts with a small group.

1. Strengths: What did your team do well?
2. Weaknesses: How did your team struggle?
3. Opportunities: What did your team accomplish? What else could it have accomplished?
4. Threats: What external problems could have hurt the team's success? Which happened and which didn't?

PREPARE TO READ

A VOCABULARY Choose **two** words that best answer the questions below.

aid (n)	combat (v)	desperate (adj)	fundamental (adj)	input (n)
campaign (n)	conservation (n)	empower (v)	inclusion (n)	judgment (n)

1. **Aid** is a form of help. What are two kinds of aid?

    a. financial   b. medical   c. entertainment

2. A **campaign** is a plan of activities designed to meet a goal. What are two kinds of campaigns?

    a. military   b. mathematical   c. political

3. To **combat** means to fight against something. What might you combat?

    a. food   b. inequality   c. crime

4. **Conservation** is the action of preserving something. What are two popular conservation initiatives?

    a. educational   b. architectural   c. environmental

5. **Desperate** means serious or hopeless. Which words often follow desperate?

    a. situation   b. outlook   c. danger

6. To **empower** someone means to enable them to achieve something. Who do many organizations often try to empower?

    a. women   b. wealthy businesspeople   c. young people

7. **Fundamental** means basic or essential. Which words often follow fundamental?

    a. luxury   b. need   c. principle

8. **Inclusion** means making a person feel that they belong. In general, which groups are often concerned about inclusion in society?

    a. elite athletes   b. people with disabilities   c. ethnic minority groups

9. **Input** is ideas or information. Which verbs often come before input?

    a. provide   b. offer   c. place

10. **Judgment** is the opinion a person reaches after careful thought. Which phrases often come before judgment?

    a. show good   b. turn down   c. question a person's

B PERSONALIZE Discuss these questions with a partner.

1. If you were planning a **campaign** to change the time your class meets, what would you do first?

2. Do you usually trust your own **judgment**? Explain.

REFLECT   Generate strategies for successful teamwork.

You are going to read about ways teams can be successful. Brainstorm physically challenging team activities such as firefighting. What strategies might the teams use to work together safely and successfully? Discuss these questions in a small group. Take notes on any teamwork strategies your group comes up with.

WORKING TOGETHER FOR SUCCESS

Rescue personnel arrive at the entrance of Tham Luang cave in Thailand.

3.2 *While financial support and strong organization are important factors in teamwork, the psychological aspects of team membership also play a role in determining success.*

1 According to an African proverb, "If you want to go fast, go alone. If you want to go far, go together." The ability to work together to accomplish a goal makes the difference between success and failure. It could even be the difference between life and death. What makes teamwork effective? Here are some **fundamental** principles of teamwork as experienced by four unique teams.

Have a clear and realistic goal

2 As a teenager, National Geographic Explorer Andrew Brennen understood the importance of education but was concerned about the way in which decisions about education were made. Andrew wanted students to have **input** into educational policy. He met several other students who shared his concerns. Andrew explains: "Our overall idea was that we students were spending 35 hours a week in the classroom, but when changes are made to the classroom, no one was asking us what worked and what didn't." The result was the Prichard Committee Student Voice Team, which quickly grew into a team of 100 students.

3 The team had a clear goal: to ensure students had a voice with regard to education. Andrew and his team have implemented[1] several strategies to meet this goal. They work together to carry out surveys, deliver workshops, give presentations, and organize events. They do much of this with the help of social media.

4 Having specific goals helped the team achieve them. One initiative was for the **inclusion** of students in selecting the school superintendents[2]. Another called for increased funding for textbooks. Andrew also led a public affairs **campaign** that resulted in $14 million in financial **aid** for students from low-income backgrounds. These initiatives were all successful because they used resources and followed plans Andrew had clearly defined from the beginning.

[1]**implement** (v) to put into effect
[2]**superintendent** (n) the manager of a school district

Develop self-respect and confidence in your team

5   In Zimbabwe, the Akashinga (a word meaning "brave ones" in the local Shona language) patrol[3] the grasslands of the Phundundu Wildlife Area to **combat** poaching, which is the illegal killing and exporting of wildlife.

6   The Akashinga are a **conservation** team with a difference: They are all women. Their founder, Damien Mander, wanted team members who were determined to make a difference; he built his team with women from difficult backgrounds. Mander put the women through a rigorous training program, which included team-building activities such as packing a 200-pound (90 kilogram) tent, dragging it up a mountain with their legs tied together, and then reassembling it. The women gained respect not only from their teammates but also from their leader. To Mander's surprise, only three of the women dropped out.

7   But perhaps most important is the self-respect these women have found. Many joined the team with little education and limited skills, but now their membership provides them with income to take care of their families and save for college. They are **empowered** to keep working toward their personal and professional goals. Member Kelly Lyee Chigumbura says, "When I manage to stop poachers, I feel accomplished . . . I want to spend my whole life here on this job, arresting poachers and protecting animals."

Focus on the goal, not on your own achievements

8   In 2018, 12 boys aged 11 to 17 and their soccer coach became lost in one of the deepest caves in Thailand. With the rainy season and floods approaching, the situation was **desperate**. A team from around the world was quickly assembled: a firefighter, a computer consultant, a retired veterinarian, and Richard Harris, a doctor and National Geographic Explorer. They had little in common apart from one thing: They were the best cave divers in the world. Their task was to find the boys and bring them to safety.

9   As the world watched, the divers worked in the flooded cave. On the 10th day, the boys were found— alive, but half a mile deep in the cave. The only way to get them out was for the divers to swim out underwater, each bringing a boy with him. As Richard Harris says, "I didn't think it would work at all . . . I put their odds of survival at zero." Miraculously, after a difficult rescue operation, all the boys and their coach were safely out of the cave.

10   Afterward, many of the divers were awarded medals. All, however, denied that they were heroes; instead, they praised the boys and the 7,000 volunteers who had been part of the operation— cooking meals, operating water pumps, or doing laundry. It was a true team effort, made possible by having one goal in mind: not heroism, not medals, but the rescue of 12 young boys.

[3]**patrol** (v) to keep watch over an area by regularly traveling around it

The Akashinga conservation team during training in Zimbabwe

Develop and show trust

11 National Geographic Explorer Hilaree O'Neill and her team of five elite mountaineers had a goal: to climb Hkakabo Razi, the highest peak in Myanmar. The journey to the summit was full of risks. To reach the mountain, the group hiked through dense jungles, crossed rivers on rope bridges, and dealt with poisonous snakes. Once on the mountain, the dangers changed to frostbite, shortages of food, and the risk of falls.

12 On the mountain, there is no alternative but to trust your team members' skills. As team member Mark Jenkins explains, "We're all roped together, so it's crucial that none of us fall. . . . You must trust your life to their **judgment** and ability, and they entrust their lives to yours." If someone does fall off a ridge while attached to a rope, the only way to save that person is for the climber behind to jump off the opposite side of the ridge to balance the fall. As Mark says, "This is the depth of trust required in mountain climbing."

13 It is also important to trust the members of the team to communicate honestly. On the day the climbers were to attempt to reach the summit, one of the climbers spoke the words they had all been thinking: "I'm scared . . . I think we should turn around." The climbers headed back down the mountain. This decision would not have been possible without trust and respect among team members.

14 An awareness of principles like these can increase team success. Andrew Brennen's team has empowered students. The work of the Akashinga has reduced elephant poaching by 80 percent in the Phundundu region of Zimbabwe. The Thai boys and their coach all emerged from the cave alive. And while the Myanmar climbers did not conquer Hkakabo Razi, their teamwork helped them to avoid a potentially fatal situation.

B MAIN IDEAS Complete the sentences in your own words.

1. Andrew Brennen was concerned about _____. One specific goal chosen by his team was _____.

2. The goal of the Akashinga is _____. Membership of the team gives women _____ and _____.

3. The situation with the Thai boys was desperate because _____. After the rescue, the divers said that _____.

4. Mountain climbers need to trust each other because _____. If a climber makes a mistake, _____.

C DETAILS Read the sentences. Write T for *True*, F for *False*, or NG for *Not Given*.

1. _____ Andrew found it difficult to attract 100 students to his team.

2. _____ Andrew Brennan and his team used social media to share their concerns.

3. _____ The Akashinga would welcome men on their team.

4. _____ Damien Mander thought many participants would not finish the training program.

5. _____ The cave rescuers were all professional divers.

6. _____ One mistake on a mountain could put other climbers' lives in danger.

CRITICAL THINKING Recognize a writer's cultural context

When you read information related to interpersonal relationships, such as "how to work on a team," keep in mind that it was probably written for a specific population. In other cultural contexts, this information may need modification or may not apply. As such, always compare the writer's cultural context with your own before deciding what to do with the information.

D APPLY Review the guidelines for working with other students at a North American university. In a small group, share whether the ideas would be applicable or not applicable to your culture. Keep track of your group's answers in the table and discuss the cultural reasons for the answers. Be ready to share what you learned with the class.

Guidelines for students in North American universities	Applicable (A) or not applicable (NA) to other cultures?
You may work in a group with students who are older than you. Students of all ages and backgrounds attend college courses.	
Your team may not have a leader. If there is a leader, it does not need to be the oldest or most experienced member.	
Everyone's opinion is equally valid. Team members may become angry if they think their ideas are being ignored.	
Communication among group members is essential. It is important to keep in regular contact and share key details with your team.	

REFLECT Design a plan that requires teamwork.

Your school has a common room where students can meet, study, and relax. This room isn't attractive, and students don't use it. You would like to make this room more appealing, so you put together a team to help you. With a small group or team, answer the questions.

1. How would your team find out what needs to change? How would your team decide what to do and where to begin?

2. What kind of specialized help would you need? Who might provide it? How would you persuade them to help?

3. How would you make sure all team members get along and reach the shared goal?

Group work prepares students for future careers.

UNIT TASK   Write an expository essay on teamwork.

You are going to write an essay giving advice on one aspect of teamwork. Use the ideas, vocabulary, and skills from the unit.

A MODEL Read the essay. Highlight the first piece of advice in each body paragraph.

How to Work on a Group Project

1   As a student, you will almost certainly have to carry out a project with a group of classmates, such as a research project, a presentation, or a written report. Many students dislike group work, saying they can produce better work on their own; they don't want their grades to be dependent on someone else's work. However, with an understanding of how groups function and strategies for making the most of group work, it is possible for even the most reluctant students to both enjoy and benefit from group projects.

2   First, think about why you are doing the group project. It's important to understand that group tasks can be useful, as they prepare students for their future careers. Whether you work in business, in health care, or in education, you will need to collaborate and complete projects with other people. Group work can help you to develop interpersonal skills and team loyalty, which are fundamental to success in the workplace. It's always a good idea to consider your academic group work as practice for your future career and do your best to improve your skills.

3   Next, look at some things you and your group can do at the beginning of the group project. A strong start will be helpful if you run into difficulties later. It's advisable to get to know your group members at the beginning so that you can share your initial thoughts on the project and plan the next steps. Exchange contact information and decide how you are going to communicate. Are you going to use email, social media, or text? You should also think about how you will get the work done, and set deadlines for each stage of the project. It's important to be very clear about who is responsible for each part of the project. If you have a team member who has good design skills, that person might be in charge of the design of the final report, for example.

4   Finally, think about ways to solve any problems between team members in the early stages. Often, difficulties in groups are caused by different personalities, so it can be helpful to learn a little about the psychology related to teamwork. Psychologists have found that there are some key roles that people may play in groups. Some roles are positive: the "initiator" suggests new ideas, the "energizer" urges the group to make a decision, and the "harmonizer" deals with disagreements among members. On the other hand, some roles are negative: the "aggressor" criticizes the work of others, and the "dominator" wants to control the group. Identify positive and negative roles early and make a plan for how to work with each. Problems can also happen when the group is not sure exactly what to do or when there is an unequal amount of work. In these cases, the worst thing is to ignore the problem and hope it disappears. It might be a good idea to talk to the other members of the group to see how everyone feels about the project. An early conversation and agreement can stop a small problem from becoming much more serious.

5   To conclude, there is no need to fear group projects as long as you follow some key tips. Recognize that group projects are great preparation for your future career. Make a strong start on the project by speaking openly and honestly with your group members. Remember that your group members bring different personalities to the project, and try to deal with any problems as soon as they occur. Keep these tips in mind, keep a positive attitude, and you may even learn to love group projects.

LEARNING TIP

English is a writer-responsible language. This means that YOU must make sure your reader understands your points. It is not the reader's responsibility to try to guess what you are trying to say. Always keep your purpose and intended audience in mind when deciding the amount of information and complexity of ideas in your writing.

B ANALYZE THE MODEL Work with a partner to complete an outline of the essay.

Introduction	Background	
	Thesis statement	
First body paragraph	Topic sentence	
	Supporting ideas/ Details	
Second body paragraph	Topic sentence	
	Supporting ideas/ Details	
Third body paragraph	Topic sentence	
	Supporting ideas/ Details	
Conclusion	Final thought	

WRITING SKILL   Paraphrase research material

When you paraphrase, you write the ideas you have found in your research in your own words. Unlike a summary, a paraphrase is around the same length as the original. You normally paraphrase single sentences or short paragraphs.

A good paraphrase does more than change vocabulary. You can, and should, change sentence structure, too.

▸ **Original:** Sieng Sokchan says, "It was hard to look for women to play this sport. First, they didn't know how to operate the wheelchairs, how to dribble the ball and shoot the ball, so they were reluctant to take part in the beginning."

▸ **Weak paraphrase:** Sieng Sokchan says it was difficult to find women to play basketball. They didn't know how to use the wheelchairs, how to move the ball and score baskets, so they were unwilling to join in the beginning.

▸ **Strong paraphrase:** Sieng Sokchan says that finding players for her team was challenging. Many of the women were hesitant, as they knew nothing about basketball and had never used a sports wheelchair.

In the weak version, the writer has changed some of the vocabulary (e.g., "hard" to "difficult," "operate" to "use"), but most of the sentence structure is exactly the same. These changes are not enough for a paraphrase and could be considered plagiarism.

C APPLY Paraphrase the statements from the readings. See Unit 2 for reporting verbs.

1. Sieng Sokchan: "Training women to this level of the game hasn't been easy. We all have different struggles and had to work harder than everyone to overcome them."

_____

_____

2. Sieng Sokchan: "The important thing is for the team to trust and believe in each other. We love each other because we are on the same team."

_____

_____

3. Andrew Brennen: "Our overall idea was that we students were spending 35 hours a week in the classroom, but when changes are made to the classroom, no one was asking us what worked and what didn't."

_____

_____

4. Richard Harris: "I didn't think [the team's plan] would work at all . . . I put [the boys'] odds of survival at zero."

_____

_____

_____

D APPLY With a partner, discuss what each statement means and which one you like the best. Then paraphrase the statements, using different words and sentence structure.

1. "Talent wins games, but teamwork and intelligence win championships." —Michael Jordan, professional basketball player

_____

_____

2. "None of us, including me, ever do great things. But we can all do small things, with great love, and together we can do something wonderful." —Mother Teresa, humanitarian

_____

_____

3. "It is amazing what you can accomplish if you do not care who gets the credit." —Harry S. Truman, past U.S. President

_____

_____

GRAMMAR   Modals and expressions for advice

Advice and suggestions can be given with modals, such as *should, ought to, have (got) to,* and *had better.*

- ▶ The students **should** put more time into their research.
- ▶ They **had better** collaborate if they want to meet their deadline.

However, sometimes these suggestions can sound too direct and strong. Softer expressions can be more appropriate when you have less authority on a topic or are writing about ideas that are not true in all situations. One way of softening advice or suggestions is to use modals of possibility, such as *may/might* and *could.*

- ▶ You **may/might** want to ask him if he needs help.
- ▶ You **might** consider giving her another opportunity.
- ▶ You **could** think about looking for a new job.

Another way to soften advice is removing "you" from the subject and focusing on the action rather than on what the person should do.

- ▶ **It can be helpful to** read the instructions before you begin.
- ▶ **It might be a good idea to** discuss the options with the team.

E GRAMMAR Rewrite the statements using softer language. There is more than one correct answer.

If you are having trouble getting along with someone on your team . . .

1. You have to invite the person for coffee.

   _____

2. You'd better hear the other person's side of the story.

   _____

3. You have to avoid blaming the other person for the problem.

   _____

4. You have got to recognize the other person's talents and strengths.

   _____

5. You ought to tell your boss.

   _____

6. You should remember the goal of the team.

   _____

F EDIT Read the email. Find and correct four errors in grammar and/or appropriateness.

Dear Valeria,

It was great to meet you at the welcome reception last week! Thank you for your email asking for suggestions on team projects. It's a good question! Here are a few tips. First of all, you'd better know exactly what you are expected to do. You ought to meet your team members for coffee at the beginning of the project. This can help you to learn about each other's strengths and weaknesses, and to plan the project. You've got to set a schedule; for example, you can decide what you want to accomplish each week. It might be a good idea to show this schedule to your professor to make sure you're on the right track. It can be helpful to remembering that everyone brings their own personality to the team. Some people are very focused, while others are more casual in their approach. Try to deal with personality problems before they get out of hand. Finally, it's a good idea to remember that team projects in college are great practice for the working world. Don't worry—you'll be fine!

Good luck,

Beth

PLAN & WRITE

G BRAINSTORM In a small group, identify two aspects of teamwork that can cause difficulties, such as dealing with personality conflicts or managing time. Take notes on why each aspect of teamwork is important and how to be successful at them. Use information from the readings and from your experiences to support your ideas.

Aspect of teamwork	This is important because . . .	How to be successful

H RESEARCH Follow the steps.

▸ Choose one aspect of teamwork from activity G to write about.
▸ Research this aspect and add notes to activity G.

I OUTLINE Complete the outline.

Title _____

Introduction

Background information _____

Thesis _____

Body paragraph 1

Topic sentence (first way to be successful) _____

Supporting ideas/Details _____

_____

Body paragraph 2

Topic sentence (second way to be successful) _____

Supporting ideas/Details _____

_____

Body paragraph 3

Topic sentence (third way to be successful) _____

Supporting ideas/Details _____

_____

Conclusion

Final thought _____

J FIRST DRAFT Use your outline to write a first draft of your essay.

K REVISE Use this list as you write your second draft.

☐ Did you include a clear thesis statement? Does everything in your essay relate to it?

☐ Did you organize your information in a logical order, with each paragraph showing a different way to build successful teamwork?

☐ Does each strategy include examples and clear reasons for doing it?

☐ Did you make sure to include only relevant information?

L EDIT Use this list as you write your final draft.

☐ Did you use appropriate expressions to introduce advice and suggestions?

☐ Did you paraphrase other people's ideas clearly and accurately?

M FINAL DRAFT Reread your essay, expand on any unclear ideas, and correct any errors. Then submit it to your teacher.

REFLECT

A Check (✓) the Reflect activities you can do and the academic skills you can use.

☐ consider what makes a team successful

☐ carry out a SWOT analysis for a team

☐ generate strategies for successful teamwork

☐ design a plan that requires teamwork

☐ write an expository essay on teamwork

☐ determine a writer's purpose and audience

☐ paraphrase research material

☐ modals and expressions for advice

☐ recognize a writer's cultural context

B Write the vocabulary words from the unit in the correct column. Add any other words that you learned. Circle words you still need to practice.

NOUN	VERB	ADJECTIVE	ADVERB & OTHER

C Reflect on the ideas in the unit as you answer these questions.

1. What is the most memorable, interesting, or helpful thing you learned in the unit?

_____

_____

2. What teamwork ideas might you use in the future?

_____

_____

3. What ideas from the unit do you want to learn more about?

_____

_____

NEW FRONTIERS IN ENGINEERING

View from the top of
the Burj Khalifa, Dubai

IN THIS UNIT

▶ Analyze what drives engineers

▶ Apply engineering concepts

▶ Evaluate engineering achievements

▶ Consider responses to engineering achievements

▶ Write a process essay describing an achievement in engineering

SKILLS

READING
Make inferences

WRITING
Describe how something was done

GRAMMAR
The passive voice to emphasize what's important

CRITICAL THINKING
Establish priorities

CONNECT TO THE TOPIC

1. Would you like to live in the Burj Khalifa, or in a similar skyscraper?

2. What do you think is the most impressive structure in the world?

A termite mound

WATCH

ARCHITECTS LEARN FROM TERMITES

A PREDICT Termites are small insects that eat wood. How do you think they inspired the design of a building without air conditioning? Watch the video and check your answer. ▶ 4.1

    a. The designer of the building copied the structures built by termites.

    b. The designer brought termites into the building to keep the air cool.

    c. The designer built the structure in a region that has many termites.

B Watch again. Complete the sentences to show how the Eastgate Centre is an example of biomimicry. ▶ 4.1

    1. The building is made of materials that can take in a lot of _____ without changing temperature.

    2. The building has small windows. This means that more heat is lost at _____, and less heat is gained during the _____.

    3. During the night, fans pull in cool night air from _____. This air moves throughout the various floors of the structure.

    4. In the morning, warm air leaves through _____ at the top of the building.

C The video ends by asking in what other ways the natural world can influence the design of buildings. Discuss ideas you have with a partner.

PREPARE TO READ

A VOCABULARY Complete the sentences with the correct form of the words.

diagonal (adj)	ensure (v)	horizontal (adj)	precaution (n)	stable (adj)
distribute (v)	foundation (n)	innovative (adj)	reinforce (v)	vertical (adj)

1. Even though igloos are made of snow, they are actually very _____.
   A well-built igloo will not collapse.

2. On a graph, the _____ line is called the x-axis and the _____
   line is the y-axis.

3. When you are using a power tool, you should wear safety glasses as a _____.

4. If engineers don't make sure the weight of a roof is evenly _____ across the entire
   structure, the heavier part can fall down.

5. The letter *X* is formed with two _____ lines.

6. Shanghai is famous for its new and _____ buildings. They are a contrast to the
   older, more traditional buildings.

7. Engineers decided to _____ the walls of the old castle with steel so that they
   would not fall down.

8. Before you remove a wall in your house, you need to _____ that it does not
   support the floor above.

9. The builders have started work on my new house! They have already laid the
   _____. The next step will be building the walls.

B PERSONALIZE Discuss these questions with a partner.

1. When you exercise or play sports, what **precautions** do you take to avoid injuries?

2. Do you know any countries whose flags have **horizontal**, **vertical**, or **diagonal** stripes? Which ones?

3. Who is the most **innovative** architect, artist, or musician that you know?

REFLECT Analyze what drives engineers.

You are going to read about some of the tallest structures in the world. Discuss in a small
group: Why do you think engineers often want to build the tallest, longest, or deepest
structure? What is gained from doing so for the following?

a. The city or region where the structure is located

b. The country where the structure is located

c. The engineers themselves

REACH FOR THE SKY

Shanghai Tower,
Shanghai, China

A PREVIEW Answer the questions.

1. Have you seen any of these buildings? Tell a partner what you know about them.

   The Burj Khalifa   The Empire State Building   Taipei 101

   The Shanghai Tower   The Riyadh Kingdom Centre   The Petronas Towers

2. What safety considerations need to be addressed when constructing a very tall building?

4.1 *How are extremely tall buildings made? Are they safe? Read the article to find out.*

1   Dubai's Burj Khalifa, Shanghai's Shanghai Tower, Kuala Lumpur's Petronas Towers, and New York City's Empire State Building are world famous for their extreme height and **innovative** designs. They have become popular tourist attractions, but they also provide much-needed residential and office space. How were these giant structures built? Are they safe? And how much higher can engineers reach?

Building a Skyscraper: How It's Done

2   While extremely high buildings vary in their design and architectural appeal, they all follow a similar construction process. First, a deep **foundation** is put in place. When you look at a skyscraper, you only see the part above the ground; what you do not see is the building's underground support, made up of **reinforced** concrete pillars. These pillars can extend up to 60 meters underground to reach the rock below. Next, **vertical** beams[1] are installed, using a crane[2]. **Horizontal** beams are then put in place to hold the building together and to **distribute** weight to the vertical columns. Sometimes, **diagonal** beams are used for extra strength. Finally, the outside walls are installed. These do not support any weight and are often covered with windows.

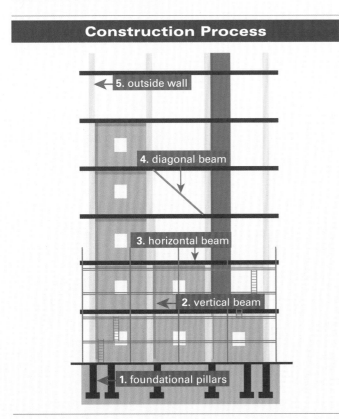

Construction Process

5. outside wall

4. diagonal beam

3. horizontal beam

2. vertical beam

1. foundational pillars

Ensuring Safety for Occupants

3   When engineering a project of such large scale, **ensuring** safety is essential. Many of the world's most famous skyscrapers play multiple roles: offices, apartment buildings, and hotels. Many have observation decks at the top. At 632 meters, the Shanghai Tower can accommodate 16,000 people every day. Engineers take many **precautions** to keep all these people safe.

4   First, skyscrapers need to be **stable**, with lower levels supporting upper levels. This requires a combination of a firm foundation and modern building materials. This is especially important for buildings such as Dubai's Burj Khalifa, which is 828 meters high and was built on weak sandstone. Engineers used a foundation of steel and concrete with 192 pillars buried over 50 meters deep underground to ensure stability. During construction, one danger was that the concrete would crack in the extreme desert heat. Since cooler concrete is less likely to crack when drying, the concrete was mixed at night when temperatures were lower. Steps like these ensure skyscrapers stand for hundreds of years.

5   Skyscrapers also need to be safe in the event of a disaster, such as a fire. In 1968, a gas explosion in an 18th-floor apartment in London destroyed an entire corner of the building, killing four people. Today, developments in engineering have led to stricter building regulations and new fire-resistant materials. It is also important that any fire does not spread; this is achieved through the use of fire doors and sprinkler systems.

6   Several of the world's tallest skyscrapers, particularly those in the Pacific Rim[3], are built in areas of heightened seismic[4] activity. Engineers have two ways to prevent buildings from collapsing during earthquakes. The first is by adding blocks of rubber to the foundation of the building. These absorb energy and reduce movement. The second is by using heavy weights at the top of the building.

[1]**beam** (n) a long piece of metal or wood, used in building

[2]**crane** (n) a tall machine used for lifting heavy items on building sites

[3]**Pacific Rim** (n) a geographical term to describe land located along the edge of the Pacific Ocean

[4]**seismic** (adj) related to the movement of Earth's crust

Minimizing Movement

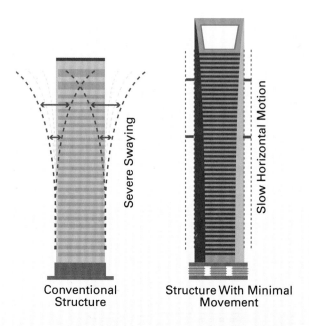

Conventional Structure

Severe Swaying

Structure With Minimal Movement

Slow Horizontal Motion

When the building is pulled in one direction by the movement of the ground, the weight brings it back to the correct position and prevents it from falling.

7   Another consideration is minimizing swaying of the building in the wind. Anyone standing on top of a skyscraper may be surprised to learn that the building moves in a strong wind. While this is normal and not dangerous, it is not a comfortable experience for people inside the building. Various methods are used to minimize movement and maintain comfort

for the occupants. Buildings that are tapered[5] at the top, such as the Burj Khalifa and Seoul's Lotte World Tower, are protected from the effects of strong winds, as are buildings with holes incorporated into the design, such as the Shanghai World Financial Center. These designs dramatically reduce the speed and force of the wind and help to reduce movement.

Ensuring Safety for Workers

8   In the 1930s, even basic safety equipment items, like hard hats, safety glasses, and safety nets, were not mandatory. Today, safety standards are much stricter. Workers have protective clothing and equipment, and they are educated on the precautions they should take when working at extreme heights. Today, deaths on construction sites are far less common than in the past.

What's Next?

9   Now that engineers have mastered the challenges of building safely into the sky, how far can they go? Right now, Saudi Arabia's Jeddah Tower is set to become the world's tallest building. While the official height is still a secret, it is expected to be over 1 kilometer tall. No one knows how long the Jeddah Tower will remain the world's tallest building, but with frequent improvements in building materials and engineering techniques, engineers really can reach for the sky.

[5]**tapered** (adj) narrower at one end than at the other

This famous photo from 1932 shows construction workers sitting on a steel beam, eating their lunches 260 meters above New York City, USA, with no safety equipment.

B MAIN IDEAS Answer the questions.

1. Which sentence best summarizes the main idea of the text?

   a. Architects and engineers always want to build the tallest and most innovative buildings, but skyscraper construction is very dangerous for those involved in the building work.

   b. Skyscrapers such as the Burj Khalifa and Shanghai Tower are incredible achievements in engineering, and their designers should be acknowledged for their vision.

   c. Modern developments in construction methods and safety measures have made it possible to build increasingly taller and safer buildings.

2. Which main ideas from the article should be included in a 100-word summary? Which details should not appear in a short summary? Write MI for *Main Ideas* or D for *Details*.

   a. _____ Tall buildings need to have very deep foundations.

   b. _____ The Burj Khalifa stands on 192 steel and concrete columns.

   c. _____ The Shanghai Tower is 632 meters tall.

   d. _____ In 1968, a gas explosion in a London skyscraper killed four people.

   e. _____ Tall buildings need special features such as weights to minimize earthquake effects and tapered design to resist strong winds.

   f. _____ Safety standards for workers on skyscraper construction sites are very strict today.

C DETAILS Underline and correct the mistakes in these sentences.

1. The foundation of a skyscraper can extend up to 15 meters under the ground.

2. When building a skyscraper, the horizontal beams are installed first.

3. The Burj Khalifa can accommodate 16,000 people every day.

4. It was safer to mix the concrete for the Burj Khalifa during the day.

5. Cities near the Atlantic Ocean are more likely to experience seismic activity.

6. Skyscrapers sway in the wind; this is very dangerous for people inside.

7. Buildings that are narrower at the top experience more negative effects from the wind.

8. The Jeddah Tower will be over 2 kilometers high.

READING SKILL   Make inferences

Inferences are assumptions you make while reading. The information is not stated directly, but you understand it to be true. Consider this example:

> Bob was part of a construction team that built some of the tallest skyscrapers in the city. He worked hundreds of feet above the ground with no safety precautions—no hard hat, no safety net. One day, he slipped on a wet, steel beam and almost fell. He was lucky, but after that, he decided to get a job on the ground. Bob never went back to the construction site, but until the day he died, he had nightmares about it.

From this text, you know *for certain*:

▶ Bob worked on a construction site with unsafe conditions.
▶ One day, he slipped on a wet, steel beam.
▶ He found a different job after that but had bad dreams for many years.

You can also *infer* the following:

▶ Safety regulations were not good enough.
▶ Bob did not fully recover psychologically from the incident.

You *cannot*, however, infer that *all* building sites were unsafe or that Bob was careless. To make an inference, there must be some support for it in the text.

D APPLY Read the paragraph and the inferences after it. Discuss with a partner which inferences are supported in the text (Y) and which are not (N). Be ready to support your answers with evidence from the text.

Built on a site just 59 feet wide, the 1,428-feet Steinway Tower in New York City is the thinnest skyscraper in the world. Designing such a narrow building was an engineering challenge. First, it was necessary to protect the Steinway Hall, a concert hall at the bottom of the skyscraper, which was built in the 1920s. The architect chose a design that reflected the style of the concert hall. In terms of safety and comfort for residents, a tapered design was used, which limits the movement of the building in the wind. Tapering the building also created outdoor areas for residents. Large windows offer amazing views over Central Park. The developers bought air rights from neighboring buildings, which prevents other buildings from increasing their height and blocking the views from the tower. Inside the building, residents have access to a gym and swimming pool. But living here is not cheap: A smaller apartment costs $14 million, and the area around the tower has been nicknamed "Billionaires' Row." This has angered New York residents, who think the city should do more to address the lack of affordable housing.

1. _____ The Steinway Tower is the tallest residential building in the world.

2. _____ The concert hall was considered an important building.

3. _____ Engineers would have preferred to demolish the concert hall.

4. _____ It is dangerous to sit outdoors during a strong wind.

5. _____ Normally, the owners of a building have the right to increase its height.

6. _____ It can be hard in New York to find a cheap place to live.

CRITICAL THINKING   Establish priorities

When completing a task, it's important to determine your priorities so that you reach your goal, avoid wasting time, and have the best possible outcome. One way is to organize your actions by how much benefit they will bring.

▶ Required actions: the minimum amount of work needed for the task to be completed correctly

▶ High-value actions: work that will greatly increase the quality or success of the task

▶ Low-value actions: work that will result in small benefits; only complete if there is time after completing other actions

---

E APPLY Imagine you work for a company that has won the contract to design a new skyscraper. Prioritize the design ideas by ranking them in order from 1 to 6 (with 1 being most important). Include your own idea. Then compare your priorities with a partner.

_____ Number and location of elevators

_____ Swimming pools, gyms, and concert halls

_____ Safety from natural disasters

_____ Balconies and roof gardens

_____ An innovative design that will give your company a good reputation

_____

REFLECT   Apply engineering concepts.

Discuss these questions in a small group.

1. Think about your own home. Do you think any of the engineering techniques in the reading were used when your home was built? Explain.

2. What safety concerns do you think were addressed when various buildings in your neighborhood were built?

PREPARE TO READ

A VOCABULARY Choose one of the words below to replace the underlined word or phrase in each sentence. Use the correct form.

address (v)	catastrophic (adj)	complication (n)	incorporate (v)	state-of-the-art (adj)
assemble (v)	civil engineer (n)	dispose of (v phr)	machinery (n)	surpass (v)

1. _____ Maggie wants to be a(n) <u>engineer who designs roads, tunnels, and bridges</u>.

2. _____ My new computer uses <u>the latest and most advanced</u> technology.

3. _____ Don't <u>throw out</u> those old magazines. They might be valuable one day.

4. _____ As a child, Adam loved heavy <u>equipment</u> used in construction, such as bulldozers, cranes, and trucks.

5. _____ The number of new buildings in the city next year is expected to <u>be greater than</u> the number this year.

6. _____ The idea of a swimming pool is a great one; it will be <u>included</u> in the design.

7. _____ We need to <u>decide what to do about</u> this problem before we can continue.

8. _____ The storm was <u>disastrous</u>. It caused a lot of damage to houses and trees.

9. _____ I've bought a new desk, but I'm not very good at <u>putting together</u> furniture. Can you help?

10. _____ <u>Problems</u> arose when the materials for the new hotel were unavailable.

B PERSONALIZE Discuss these questions with a partner.

1. Do you like to **assemble** things? If so, what have you assembled? If not, why not?
2. Describe a problem or challenge that you had to **address** recently. What happened?
3. What is the most **state-of-the-art** device that you own? What makes it special?

> **REFLECT** Evaluate engineering achievements.
>
> You are going to read about a tunnel. Think of any structures that connect people in two places; for example people on two sides of a river, people on an island, or even people in two countries. Discuss these questions with a partner.
>
> 1. What are the economic, political, and social advantages of building new, efficient ways for people to travel between places?
> 2. Are there any disadvantages of enabling increased travel between regions?

ENGINEERING MIRACLE
UNDER THE SEA

The English Channel separates England and France.

■ 4.2 Building high above the ground is an engineering challenge, but what about building deep below the sea? Tunnels are equally challenging to design and construct—especially when they run underwater.

1   For anyone standing on the cliffs of southern England or northern France, it would be hard to believe what lies below. Beneath the fishing boats, seagulls, and gentle waves lies one of the greatest engineering achievements the world has ever seen: the Channel Tunnel. The American Society of Civil Engineers has named the Channel Tunnel one of the Seven Wonders of the Modern World—and with good reason. A 50-kilometer tunnel connecting England and France, the Channel Tunnel is the longest underwater tunnel in the world.

2   Since the Ice Age, the British Isles have been separated from their European neighbors, and engineers over the years have been inspired to find ways to connect the two land masses. The idea for a tunnel under the sea first came up as early as 1802, proposed by French engineer Albert Mathieu, but at that time, the technology to build one did not exist. It was not until the 1980s, prompted by increased commerce between the two countries, that an agreement was reached.

3   Building a long tunnel always presents challenges—but as **civil engineer** Lucy Rew says, "Engineers love a challenge." Before construction could begin, some important decisions were made. It was decided that two parallel railway tunnels 7.6 meters in diameter would be built, together with a smaller service tunnel. This service tunnel would be used to build the main tunnels and would later be used for maintenance. The three tunnels would be built in the chalk layer below the sea bed; at their deepest point, these tunnels are 75 meters deep. The three tunnels would be built from both the English and the French side, and they would meet in the middle at the end of construction.

4   The next step was to determine the **machinery** to be used. Teams needed to cut through the rock below the sea bed. Eleven tunnel boring[1] machines (TBMs) were developed at a cost of several million dollars each. Each one was up to 243 meters long and had a head 15 meters in diameter[2], which cut through the rock. The edges of the head were made of tungsten carbide, one of the hardest materials in the world. **Incorporated** into each TBM was a conveyor belt[3]. This carried away the rock that was dug out by the TBM. The rock was then placed on trains in the service tunnel and delivered to sites on land, where it was **disposed of** safely. This process allowed engineers to clear, on average, 149 meters of rock every week. Safety concerns were **addressed** from the outset. The pressure from the sea above meant that there was a risk of water flowing into the tunnel which would have been **catastrophic**. To counter this danger, the TBMs were waterproof, so anyone working inside the TBM would be protected.

5   Construction began in 1988, with work starting on both sides. The first tunnel to be built was the service tunnel. Eleven TBMs were then **assembled** below the ground; this process took several months. **Complications** arose when fault lines[4] were found in the chalk on the French side, which allowed water to leak into the tunnel and which interfered with construction. Emergency waterproofing measures were taken. When the tunnel was complete, its walls were lined with slabs[5] made of concrete and steel rods. These slabs form a protective barrier between the sea and the people in the tunnel. The final stage was laying the tracks for both passenger and cargo trains.

6   Since construction started at both ends, the English and French teams had to be careful to stay on course, as they needed to meet in the middle. Would the two tunnels meet? This was the big question, and

---

[1]**bore** (v) to make a hole in something with a tool or by digging

[2]**diameter** (n) a straight line passing through the center of a body or figure, especially a circle or sphere

[3]**conveyor belt** (n) a moving band designed to move items from one place to another

[4]**fault line** (n) a break in Earth's surface

[5]**slab** (n) a thick, flat piece of stone, concrete, or wood

it was answered in October 1990. The British and French tunnels were almost perfectly aligned, with only a 50-centimeter difference that caused no problems. On December 1, 1990, Philippe Cozette from France and Graham Fagg from England shook hands underneath the English Channel with the world's media watching. Cozette called the event "a fabulous moment," while Fagg said it was "history made." Cozette and Fagg remained friends for many years afterward.

7   However, the construction of the Channel Tunnel also had its dark moments. Over 13,000 workers were involved in the project: engineers, geologists, construction experts, technicians, laborers, and many more. Twelve of them lost their lives; the first was 19-year-old Andrew McKenna, who was hit by a train carrying rock. As a *Construction News* report stated at the time, "The loss of those lives must always be in the minds of people involved in the project, particularly when celebrating the project's successes."

8   Finally, nearly 200 years after Albert Mathieu's vision, the Channel Tunnel was opened on May 6, 1994. Today, 20 million business travelers and tourists use the tunnel every year, traveling from London to Paris in less than two and a half hours, which includes 35 minutes under the channel. In addition, **state-of-the-art** cargo trains carry 1.6 million trucks through the tunnel every year, avoiding the need for slower and weather-dependent transportation by ship.

9   The Channel Tunnel has passed its 25th anniversary, and the question of what comes next remains. While the Channel Tunnel remains the world's longest underwater tunnel, it is not the world's longest tunnel, or even its deepest. The Channel Tunnel has been **surpassed** in length and depth by the Gotthard Base Tunnel in Switzerland, which opened in 2016 and passes under the Swiss Alps for 57 kilometers. With increasing concerns about the environmental effects of air travel, underground railways, which emit up to 90 percent fewer greenhouse gases, might be the way of the future.

The Channel Tunnel under construction

B MAIN IDEAS Order the information as it appears in the reading (1–7).

_____ Complications arose when leaks appeared in the tunnel walls.

_____ Philippe Cozette and Graham Fagg met in the middle.

_____ The tunnel was opened in 1994.

_____ Engineers decided to build three tunnels.

_____ The idea to build a tunnel under the English Channel has a long history.

_____ Twelve workers lost their lives during the construction of the tunnel.

_____ Special tunnel-boring machines were developed.

C DETAILS Write T for _True_, F for _False_, or NG for _Not Given_ for each sentence.

1. _____ It is more difficult to build a tunnel under the sea than under a land mass.

2. _____ The main motivation for building the tunnel was an increase in trade.

3. _____ Europe already had suitable machinery for building tunnels.

4. _____ The service tunnel is bigger than the railway tunnels.

5. _____ The threat of water in the tunnel was a serious concern.

6. _____ Philippe Cozette and Graham Fagg were senior members of their teams.

7. _____ It is cheaper to travel by rail through the tunnel than to travel by plane.

8. _____ The Channel Tunnel is the longest tunnel in the world.

READING TIP

When you are reading, don't ignore pictures and diagrams. Diagrams can give you a lot of important information. When you see a diagram in a reading, think about why it has been included and what you can learn from it.

D Look at the diagram. What does it tell you about the Channel Tunnel that was not included in the reading? Discuss the questions with a partner.

1. How many ways are there to access the tunnel? Where are they, and what are they called? _____

2. Is the meeting point in the middle, or closer to one of the countries?

   _____

3. What other tunnel was planned for under the channel? Where would it begin and end? _____

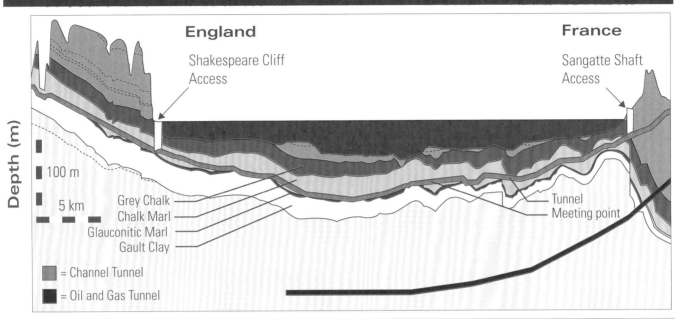

The Channel Tunnel

England — Shakespeare Cliff Access

France — Sangatte Shaft Access

Depth (m)

100 m

5 km

Grey Chalk
Chalk Marl
Glauconitic Marl
Gault Clay

Tunnel
Meeting point

■ = Channel Tunnel
■ = Oil and Gas Tunnel

REFLECT Consider responses to engineering achievements.

Philippe Cozette and Graham Fagg considered the completion of the Channel Tunnel to be a great historic event. Some people might agree; some might not. It depends on their position, which can often be influenced by political views and personal experience. Work with a partner to complete the table.

	Who might say this?	Why?
"It was a miracle of engineering!"	1.	
	2.	
	3.	
	Who might say this?	Why?
"It was a waste of time and money!"	1.	
	2.	
	3.	

The Golden Gate Bridge,
San Francisco, California, USA

| UNIT TASK | Write a process essay describing an achievement in engineering. |

You are going to research and write a short essay about the building of a remarkable structure. Use the ideas, vocabulary, and skills from the unit.

A MODEL Read the essay. Why was this bridge considered "impossible" to build?

The "Impossible Bridge": Building the Golden Gate Bridge

1 Countless movies have been filmed there, couples have been married there, and millions of photographs have been taken there. San Francisco's Golden Gate Bridge has been named one of the Wonders of the Modern World by the American Society of Civil Engineers, and it is one of the best-known bridges in the world. This world-famous bridge, once called the "impossible bridge," was a miracle of engineering when it was built in the 1930s.

2 Building a bridge across the San Francisco Bay was not an easy task. The bridge was first considered necessary in the early 20th century because the city of San Francisco sits on a peninsula and was isolated from the surrounding communities. However, there were several obstacles to completing the project. The water in San Francisco Bay is deep and muddy. The bay also has high winds, strong currents, and dense fog. Even worse, California is at risk of seismic activity. Many experts were skeptical about trying to build a bridge in this environment.

3   In 1917, however, engineer Joseph Strauss made plans for a bridge and assured city officials that he could build it within budget. Construction began in 1933. First, concrete blocks were sunk deep into the earth at both ends of the bridge. These blocks provided foundations designed to withstand earthquakes. On top of these blocks, towers were built, which carried the weight of the bridge. Next, cables were installed between the towers. Steel posts were suspended from the cables, and the base for the road surface was attached to these. Finally, the road was installed and the bridge was painted. The famous orange color was chosen by architect Irving Morrow. He chose a color that would be visible in San Francisco's foggy weather.

4   Throughout the process, several safety measures were put in place. For one of the first times on a construction site, workers were required to wear hard hats. In addition, a safety net was installed in case any worker fell. Many workers did fall and were saved by the net. Despite these measures, 10 people were killed when they fell together from the bridge, and the net could not support their weight.

5   The Golden Gate Bridge was officially opened on May 27, 1937 to huge excitement. At 2,737 meters long and 227 meters above sea level, it was the longest and tallest suspension bridge in the world. Since that day, over 2 billion vehicles have passed over the bridge, which successfully connects San Francisco with neighboring towns. Today, newer bridges in China, Japan, France, and other parts of the world are longer and taller than the Golden Gate. However, it remains a famous symbol and a sign of hope for newcomers to California.

B ANALYZE THE MODEL Find the following sentences in the essay. Add the time expression used by the writer.

1. _____, however, engineer Joseph Strauss made plans for a bridge and assured city officials that he could build it within budget.

2. _____, concrete blocks were sunk deep into the earth at both ends of the bridge.

3. _____, the road was installed and the bridge was painted.

4. _____, several safety measures were put in place.

5. _____, over 2 billion vehicles have passed over the bridge.

C ANALYZE THE MODEL Work with a partner to complete an outline of the model.

Title		
Introduction	Background	
	Thesis statement	
First body paragraph	Topic sentence	
	Supporting ideas/Details	
Second body paragraph	Topic sentence	
	Supporting ideas/Details	
Third body paragraph	Topic sentence	
	Supporting ideas/Details	
Conclusion	Final thought	

WRITING SKILL   Describe how something was done

Describing a process or how something is done is common in academic writing. You might be asked to describe the steps in a marketing plan, or in a science experiment. When you describe how something was done, there are several things to keep in mind:

1. Give the history or background of the project, or the reason behind it. Predict what your reader will want to know. Leave your reader eager to learn more but not lacking basic facts.
2. Organize your essay chronologically. You are telling a story. Start with the origins of the project, and then outline the key points in its completion. Finally, talk about the use and status of the project today.
3. Use time expressions such as: *first*, *next*, *later*, and so on. Or use prepositional phrases such as: *After several years of negotiation*, or *For the first time on a construction site*. These expressions will make your writing easier to follow.
4. Use the passive voice to emphasize what's important. For example, in the sentence, "The Golden Gate Bridge was built in the 1930s," the emphasis is on the bridge.

D APPLY Read the paragraph and work with a partner to identify the items below.

The Aswan Dam

The Aswan Dam in Egypt is the world's largest dam. Built across the Nile River, it was designed to control flooding and to provide energy. After 11 years of construction, the dam was completed on July 21, 1970. Although it is relatively new, many attempts have been made to build a dam across the Nile. First, there was an attempt in the 11th century, but it was unsuccessful. Later there were several more attempts, including one that was completed in 1902, but it, too, proved unsuccessful at controlling the floods. Today, the dam has an impact on the local economy, as it is successful in controlling flooding and in providing energy. It is also a popular tourist attraction.

▸ Information that tells the history or background of the project

_____

_____

_____

▸ Time expressions and prepositional phrases of time

_____

▸ The passive voice to emphasize what's important in a sentence

_____

E NOTICE THE GRAMMAR Discuss with a partner which of the two sentences is more appropriate and why.

1. Next, the vertical beams are installed, using a crane.
   Next, construction workers install the vertical beams, using a crane.

2. Would the two tunnels meet? This was the big question, and it was answered in October 1990.
   Would the two tunnels meet? This was the big question, and people answered it in October 1990.

The Aswan Dam, Egypt

GRAMMAR The passive voice to emphasize what's important

When you want to emphasize the person or thing the action happens to (the receiver), and not the person or thing performing the action (the agent), use the passive voice (*be* + past participle of the verb). If you want to mention a specific person or thing responsible for the action, use a *by* phrase. Note that the form of *be* shows the time.

Present:	The building **is used** by 3 million people every day.
	The palace gardens **are surrounded** by a high wall.
	Is photography **permitted** in the building?
Simple past:	The bridge **was opened** in 2011.
	Many precautions **were taken** to keep workers safe.
	Was the structure **damaged** by the earthquake?
Present perfect:	The Panama Canal **has been expanded** to make it wider.
	Countless films **have been filmed** there.
	Has the design of the building **been approved**?

F GRAMMAR Use the prompts to make passive sentences in the past.

When the skyscraper was built, . . .

1. engineers / choose / construction site _____

2. raise / money _____

3. architects / select / design of building _____

4. dig / foundation _____

5. implement / safety measures _____

6. construct / steel framework _____

7. install / outside walls _____

8. put in place / elevators _____

9. design team / paint / walls _____

10. sell / apartments _____

G EDIT Read the paragraph. Find and correct four errors with the use of the passive voice.

Fort Knox: A Restricted Building

Fort Knox is located in Kentucky in the United States. It is a storage facility for gold and other valuable items that belong to the U.S. government. Fort Knox was constructed in the 1930s and is one of the most secure buildings on Earth. It is build with concrete, steel, and granite. Because the building was designed to store precious items, an extensive network of alarms and video cameras was installing. The doors are 21 inches thick and made of fire-resistant metals. Today, the building is surround by electric fences and is heavily guarded. If you travel to the United States on vacation, don't try to visit Fort Knox: Tourists not allowed to enter the building.

PLAN & WRITE

H BRAINSTORM Work in a small group. Choose three famous structures. You can choose buildings, tunnels, bridges, dams, roads, or other structures. Complete the table with information about each one. See how much you already know without looking anything up.

Name of structure			
Where is it?			
When and why was it built?			
Records held (longest, highest, etc.)			
Construction challenges			
What do people think about it?			
Other interesting facts			

I RESEARCH Follow the steps.

► Research your three structures and add to your notes in activity H.

► Decide which structure you want to write about in your essay.

WRITING TIP

When you research and copy exact words from a source, these words might later appear in your essay with no quotation marks. This is called accidental plagiarism. To avoid this, take notes in your own words. With basic information, such as the height of a building, just write down the numbers. Never copy sentences directly, even early in the writing process. Note where the information came from so that you can cite it later.

J OUTLINE Complete the outline.

Title _____

Introduction

Background information _____

Thesis _____

Body paragraph 1

Main point _____

Supporting ideas/Details _____

Body paragraph 2

Main point _____

Supporting ideas/Details _____

Body paragraph 3

Main point _____

Supporting ideas/Details _____

Conclusion

Final thought _____

K FIRST DRAFT Use your outline to write a first draft of your essay.

L REVISE Use this list as you write your second draft.

☐ Did you give basic information about your structure (e.g., location, size, length, age)?

☐ Did you explain any challenges there were in building your structure?

☐ Did you describe what makes this structure notable?

☐ Did you follow a logical, chronological order?

☐ Did you use time expressions to connect events to each other?

☐ Did you make sure to only include relevant information?

M EDIT Use this list as you write your final draft.

☐ Did you use verbs correctly, especially past and present forms?

☐ Did you use the passive voice correctly to emphasize objects?

N FINAL DRAFT Reread your essay and correct any errors. Then submit it to your teacher.

REFLECT

A Check (✓) the Reflect activities you can do and the academic skills you can use.

- ☐ analyze what drives engineers
- ☐ apply engineering concepts
- ☐ evaluate engineering achievements
- ☐ consider responses to engineering achievements
- ☐ write a process essay describing an achievement in engineering

- ☐ make inferences
- ☐ describe how something was done
- ☐ the passive voice to emphasize what's important
- ☐ establish priorities

B Write the vocabulary words from the unit in the correct column. Add any other words that you learned. Circle words you still need to practice.

NOUN	VERB	ADJECTIVE	ADVERB & OTHER

C Reflect on the ideas in the unit as you answer these questions.

1. Will this unit make you feel differently the next time you enter a skyscraper, drive through a tunnel, or cross a bridge? Explain why.

2. What was the most memorable, interesting, or helpful thing you learned in the unit?

3. What ideas from the unit do you want to learn more about? Explain why.

UNIT 5

WALL ART

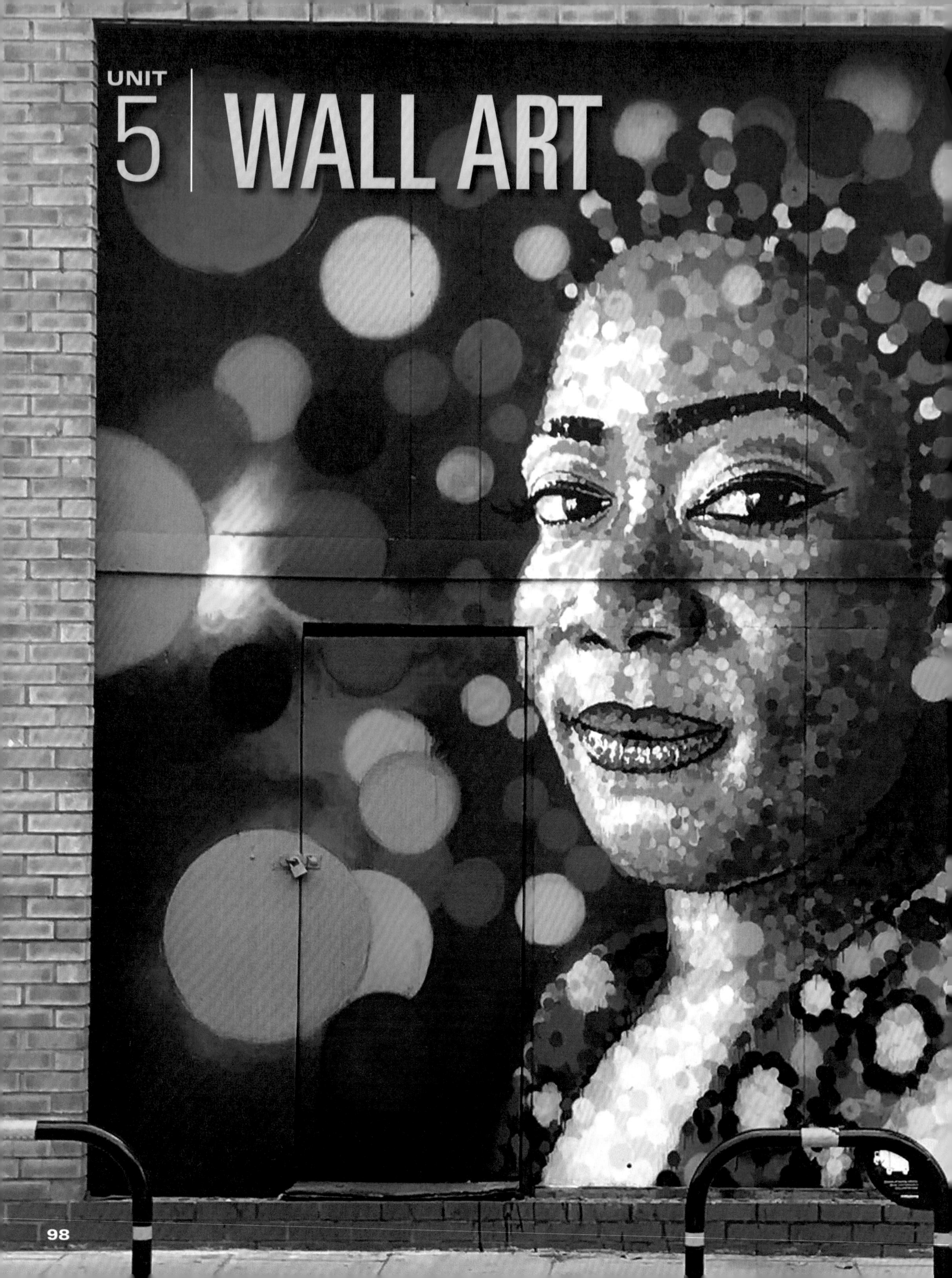

Portrait of Theresa
by James Cochran,
known as Jimmy C,
London, England

No loading
at any time

JIMMY. C.

CONNECT TO THE TOPIC

1. How might art like this impact the neighborhood it's in?

2. Do you enjoy looking at art? What kind of art do you like?

WATCH

COUNTER **MAPPING**

Prehistoric
Zuni caves,
New Mexico, USA

A PREVIEW Answer the questions with a partner. ▶ 5.1

1. What is the purpose of a map?

2. *Counter* means to go against, or to do something in response to something. What do you think *counter mapping* means?

3. Watch the video. What is different about Jim Enote's maps?

B Watch again. Choose the correct answers, according to Jim Enote. Then discuss what he means by each statement. ▶ 5.1

1. More lands have been lost to native peoples probably through **map making / conflict with non-native people**.

2. In deciding to make maps, Jim was more concerned about **geographical accuracy / relevance to the Zuni people**.

3. The maps allow the Zuni people to **start talking about their cultural history / educate their children about the geography of the United States**.

4. If Jim's grandparents could see the maps, they would **not understand them / recognize the places and stories shown**.

C PERSONALIZE Enote's maps tell us a lot about the Zuni way of life. What might a Zuni-style map of your town look like? What would be included?

PREPARE TO READ

A VOCABULARY Complete the sentences with the correct form of the words.

archaeology (n)	compile (v)	distorted (adj)	the latter (n phr)	random (adj)
classify (v)	consensus (n)	extinct (adj)	parallel (adj)	speculate (v)

1. Looking at some modern art, you might think the artist threw _____ colors and shapes onto the canvas. This is not usually the case; there is usually planning involved.

2. Ken has _____ a list of paintings he would like to see when he travels to Paris.

3. The highway runs _____ to the river; you can see the river beside the road.

4. We visited two museums in Paris, one with ancient art and one with modern art. I preferred _____, as I am interested in new and innovative uses of color.

5. The ostrich is _____ as a bird, even though it cannot fly.

6. Some animals, such as the rhinoceros, the tiger, and the snow leopard, are in danger of becoming _____ unless action is taken to save them.

7. Nancy is working on her master's degree in _____. She's going to Peru next summer to try to find evidence of the earliest people in the country.

8. No one really knows who painted the world's oldest art. We can only _____.

9. In abstract art, figures are often _____, unlike in more realistic art where shapes look accurate.

10. Sadly, the school district has not been able to reach a _____ on the value of art in the curriculum. Some schools teach art, while others do not.

B PERSONALIZE Discuss these questions with a partner.

1. If you **compiled** a list of places you would like to visit, what would be on your list?
2. Talk about a time when you and other people, such as your classmates, friends, or family, had to reach a **consensus** on something. What happened?

REFLECT   Consider the value of art from the past.

Before you read about some of the oldest art on Earth, discuss the questions in a small group.

1. What can we learn from looking at art from the past?
2. What countries or regions are rich in ancient art?
3. If you could go back in time and talk to an artist, who would you talk to? What would you ask?

PAINTING
PREHISTORY

A PREVIEW Look at the photo and read the title and subheadings. Answer the questions. After reading, check your predictions.

1. How old do you think these paintings are?

2. Why were they painted?

1   On September 12, 1940, a French teenager named Marcel Ravidat was taking his dog for a walk, when the dog fell down a hole. Marcel found the dog, and in doing so, he found something else: the entrance to a cave. Returning later with three friends to explore, Marcel discovered that the walls of the cave were covered with paintings. Marcel and his friends had accidentally discovered one of the greatest finds in **archaeology** of the 20th century: the Lascaux cave system in southwestern France.

2   When investigated by experts, the Lascaux caves were found to contain over 6,000 paintings, some of them 16 feet (5 meters) long. Archaeologists believe that these paintings were created 17,000 years ago by seminomadic[1] tribespeople. Similar cave systems would later be discovered elsewhere in France and Spain. Today, Lascaux is one of over 400 known "decorated caves" in Europe, and similar caves have been found on every continent except Antarctica. There is a remarkable similarity in the paintings found in various caves around the world: Animals, human hands, and abstract shapes are common.

What is shown in the Lascaux paintings?

3   The cave paintings at Lascaux mainly show animals running, jumping, eating, or lying on the ground. The animals are ones the early Europeans would have hunted, including lions, wild horses, bison, mountain goats, and deer. In some cases, the paintings give information about creatures now **extinct**, such as the auroch (the ancestor of the modern cow) and the mammoth (part of the elephant family). Self-portraits, unfortunately, were not common; there is only one human among the 6,000 paintings at Lascaux. Some caves elsewhere do contain paintings of human figures, usually hunting, but unlike the animal paintings, these were not painted in detail. They often resemble stick figures and do not have faces. Also missing at Lascaux are paintings of trees, flowers, and other plants. We can only **speculate** about what this means; perhaps the lack of human figures and plants in the cave paintings tells us something about the importance of humans compared to animals. Interestingly, Lascaux does contain many paintings of human hands and abstract symbols, such as **parallel** lines, dots, circles, stars, and arrows. The meaning of these drawings is also a mystery.

[1]**seminomadic** (adj) living in temporary homes and moving seasonally

The Great Hall of the Bulls in Lascaux, France

Hand shapes and animals
on a cave wall

How were these paintings made?

4   An analysis of the Lascaux cave paintings shows
that the early painters used some complex art
techniques. The painters made paint by pressing
stones to make powders and adding liquid. Over
100 stones in various shades of red, yellow, brown,
and black have been found at Lascaux. The painters
did not use blue or green, perhaps because they
lacked the resources to make these colors. Painting
techniques commonly used included spitting the
paints or blowing them through a hollow bone to
create stencil[2] drawings. A modern way would be to
blow paint through a straw over an object. Ancient
painters would often place their hands on the
wall and blow paint over them. When the painters
removed their hands, they had perfect human hand
shapes on their walls. Spots were formed with tools
made of rolled animal skins; multiple spots were
then used to form outlines of large animals, and
some paintings were "signed" with a row of blow-
painted spots. Other tools included brushes made
from horsehair, and sharp stones, which were used to
cut lines into the white rock. **The latter** were used
for small details, such as eyes.

5   We know from the Lascaux paintings that our
ancestors had a basic understanding of perspective[3].
Where animals were painted high on a wall, they were
purposely painted in such a way that when viewed
from close up, they appear **distorted**, but when
viewed from ground level, they appear normal. In
some cases, creatures appear too long when viewed
close up, but are a normal length when seen from the
center of the cave.

Why were they painted?

6   Cave painting was clearly time-consuming and at
times physically challenging. In some caves, painted
areas could only be reached by crawling through
narrow passageways that artists could barely fit
through; other paintings were drawn using ladders
made of tree trunks or ropes made of twisted plants.
So, why were they made? There is no **consensus**
on this. Some researchers believe they were painted
for ceremonies that took place in the caves. Perhaps

[2]**stencil** (n) a design made by placing an item on a
 surface and painting around it

[3]**perspective** (n) the placement of objects in a painting
 or drawing to show depth and distance

early humans painted animals to give themselves strength before hunting. Another theory is that the different animals and abstract shapes were symbols of specific tribes or social groups. Pairs of animals, such as horse and cow, could have symbolized the joining together of two groups, perhaps in a form of marriage. The paintings might also have been made to tell stories, communicating the successes and failures of earlier hunts.

What about the abstract shapes?

7   While most of the research into early cave painting has focused on the pictures of animals, the most interesting studies in recent years have been related to the nonanimal shapes. At many cave sites, the various lines, circles, and spots far outnumber the animal images. Researchers have **compiled** lists of the symbols found in caves across Europe. They have found that over a period of 30,000 years and across the entire continent of Europe, only 32 distinct symbols appear on cave walls. Similar shapes have also been found in caves in various parts of the world. If these were **random** drawings or decorations, there would be more variation. Instead, the same signs repeat across different people, locations, and time periods. This suggests that the shapes had a meaning beyond just decoration.

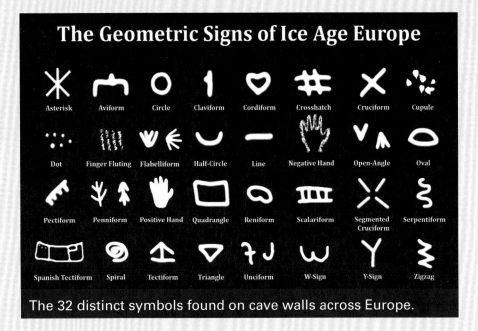

The 32 distinct symbols found on cave walls across Europe.

The system of symbols is not large enough to be **classified** as a written language or alphabet, but these shapes almost certainly symbolize something, such as weapons, early counting, or geographical features like lakes, rivers, or mountains.

8   Research into the cave art of our ancestors continues, and scientists continue to make exciting discoveries. It seems that the field of archaeology is on the verge of[4] a number of important breakthroughs which will teach us more about how our ancestors communicated through painting.

---

[4]**on the verge of** (phr) at the point when something is about to happen

B MAIN IDEAS Complete this brief summary of the article with your own words.

At Lascaux, France, over [1]_____ paintings were found in caves. Most

of the paintings show pictures of [2]_____, such as lions and horses.

They were painted with paints made from red, yellow, brown, and black stones. Researchers

are not sure exactly why the paintings were made, especially as many are located in places

that are [3]_____. One possible explanation for their existence

is [4]_____. Today, some of the most interesting research is on

the [5]_____ shapes on the walls of the caves.

C DETAILS Choose the correct word or phrase to complete each sentence.

1. The paintings in the caves were made around _____ years ago.
   a. 1,700   b. 17,000   c. 170,000

2. The largest paintings are _____ long.
   a. 1.6 feet (0.5 meters)   b. 16 feet (5 meters)   c. 160 feet (50 meters)

3. In the 6,000 paintings, there is only one _____.
   a. human   b. type of animal   c. color

4. One paint color not used by the cave painters was _____.
   a. yellow   b. red   c. blue

5. Modern archaeologists have _____ about why these paintings were made.
   a. several theories   b. no idea   c. a clear understanding

6. The abstract shapes found in various caves are _____.
   a. random drawings   b. consistent   c. a system of writing

---

READING SKILL **Distinguish facts from opinions**

Facts can be checked. They include numbers, such as population and size, dates and other historical information, and proven information about science and nature.

Opinions cannot be checked. If something cannot be known for sure or is debatable, it's an opinion. If it's a prediction about the future, it's also probably an opinion. An opinion from an expert can help a writer's argument, but it is still an opinion. Read critically to distinguish facts from opinions and decide how reliable the information is. The following features can indicate an opinion.

- ▸ Verbs that show uncertainty, such as *think*, *believe*, or *speculate*
- ▸ Modals that indicate possibility, such as *might*, *may*, *could*, or *should*
- ▸ Adjectives suggesting a personal reaction, such as *interesting*, *boring*, or *important*

D APPLY Read the statements and write F for *Fact* or O for *Opinion*. Underline the piece of information that helped you choose your answer.

1. _____ Archaeologists believe that these paintings were created 17,000 years ago by seminomadic tribespeople.

2. _____ Today, Lascaux is one of over 400 known "decorated caves" in Europe, and similar caves have been found on every continent except Antarctica.

3. _____ There is only one human among the 6,000 paintings at Lascaux.

4. _____ While most of the research into early cave painting has focused on the pictures of animals, the most interesting studies in recent years have been related to the nonanimal shapes.

5. _____ Another theory is that the different animals and abstract shapes were symbols of specific tribes or social groups.

CRITICAL THINKING   Evaluate evidence for theories

Some statements are clearly facts; others are clearly opinions. Some opinions, such as those from experts, may be more reliable than others. Often you will come across information that makes you think, "I think this is true . . . it seems to be true . . . but I need more evidence." This evidence could take the form of written documentation, reliable reports from others, discoveries, or personal observation.

For example, researchers into ancient history might suspect that a certain society lived in family units, but they have no reliable evidence. When cave drawings of family units are discovered, the researchers have the evidence they were looking for. When you see a statement that *seems* to be true, ask yourself what more you would need to know before you can treat it as a fact.

E APPLY Look at the following theories about people from the time of the Lascaux cave paintings. Since there are no written records from this time period, we need to look for other kinds of evidence. What evidence might be discovered that would classify these as facts? There are no right or wrong answers.

Theory	Evidence needed
The cave painters did not actually live in caves.	
The cave painters traveled long distances every year.	
The cave painters' survival depended on successful hunting.	
The written symbols of the cave painters originated in Africa.	

REFLECT   Discuss issues around studying early art.

Researchers continue to learn more about our early ancestors through investigations of their art. Discuss the questions in a small group.

1. What is the value of this research? How can we use the information that is uncovered?

2. How should this kind of research be funded? By governments? Universities? Private organizations?

3. The Lascaux caves are no longer open to the public, but an exact replica or copy has been built. Why do you think the caves are no longer open? Would you be interested in visiting the replica? Explain.

PREPARE TO READ

A VOCABULARY Choose the correct meaning for the word in bold.

1. The idea that street painting is a true form of art is gaining **acceptance** in the art world.

   a. agreement   b. disagreement   c. confusion

2. Some **affluent** art collectors helped the artist to establish his own studio.

   a. generous   b. rich   c. poor

3. **Consumerism** among teenagers is growing. Some people think this is a problem because it suggests teens value goods over more important things, such as relationships.

   a. gaming   b. a computer program   c. an increasing consumption of goods

4. **Inevitably**, the film was not a success as the subject was not of interest to a wide audience.

   a. unavoidably   b. surprisingly   c. frequently

5. One **interpretation** of the novel is that the author was writing about his childhood.

   a. judgment   b. explanation   c. response

6. What is the company's **policy** on taking vacation time? Can we take it at any time?

   a. permission   b. style   c. rule

7. Although the painting is not signed, experts **presume** that it was painted by van Gogh, as it shows his distinct use of color.

   a. know   b. guess   c. understand

8. Several **prominent** Chinese artists combine western and eastern themes in their work.

   a. well-known   b. well-liked   c. unknown

9. Do you like this picture on my wall? It's a Picasso **reproduction**.

   a. original painting   b. copy   c. statue

10. Some art critics admire Banksy's talent; others say his work is **vandalism** and should be removed.

    a. bad use of public space   b. great art   c. destruction of property

B PERSONALIZE Discuss these questions with a partner.

1. Who are the most **prominent** artists in your country? What do you think of their work?

2. Is **consumerism** a concern in your country? If so, what can be done to address the problem? If not, why do you think your country is not affected?

3. What is your school's **policy** on absences?

REFLECT   Form an opinion about modern street painting.

Before you read about street art, imagine you are walking through your town or city and you see someone painting a flower on the side of a building. Discuss the questions in a small group.

1. Would you consider the painting to be a form of art, or would you consider it vandalism?

2. Would your answer to question 1 be different if the picture were of something related to violence or a negative image of a group of people?

Wall art by Xavier Prou, known as
Blek le Rat, Dubai, United Arab Emirates

MAKING A STATEMENT, ONE WALL AT A TIME

A PREVIEW Look at the photo. Answer the questions.

1. What message do you think this artist is sending through this painting?
2. Why do you think the artist chose to paint on a wall?

5.2 *The earliest humans painted on cave walls. Thousands of years later, humans are still painting on walls. Only this time, their walls are in cities, their paint comes in spray cans, and their goal is to make a statement about contemporary society.*

1   In late 2020, a painting called *Aachoo!!* appeared on the wall of a house in Bristol, England. An elderly woman is shown sneezing so hard that she has dropped her bag and walking stick, and her false teeth are flying through the air. The message was clear: Stay healthy this winter. The artist? The world's most **prominent** street artist, Banksy.

2   The artist who calls himself Banksy is well known for his stenciled artwork that appears overnight on the sides of buildings, on bridges, and even on public transportation around the world. Yet the man himself is a mystery, as the identity of Banksy has remained a secret since he started painting in the 1990s. What is known is that he puts a lot of effort into creating his works and that he uses his work to express his opinions about society. Here are three examples:

POLLARD ST

Yellow Lines Flower Painter by Banksy

▶ *Very Little Helps* shows three children pledging allegiance[1] to a flag, which is actually a plastic bag from a well-known supermarket chain. A common **interpretation** is that Banksy wanted to comment on **consumerism** and how it starts at an early age.

▶ *Yellow Lines Flower Painter* shows a city employee taking a break from his job. His job is to paint yellow "no-parking" lines along the side of a street, but he has used his yellow paint to create a simple flower on the side of a building. Banksy's message: Don't be afraid to express your creativity.

▶ *Season's Greetings* appeared overnight on the wall of a garage in a steel manufacturing town in Wales. The painting appears to show a small boy enjoying a snowfall and trying to catch snowflakes on his tongue. A closer look reveals the "snow" to be ash from an industrial waste bin painted on another wall. We can **presume** that Banksy wanted to draw attention to the severe air pollution in the town.

Other Bansky works have protested against global warming, the treatment of refugees, and the testing of beauty products on animals.

3 Banksy may be the world's most famous street artist, but he is not the only one. In cities around the world, artists are using cans of spray paint to make statements about society or the environment in public spaces. For example, in France, Xavier Prou, who paints under the name Blek le Rat, paints images of marginalized[2] members of society, such as beggars, on the sides of buildings to raise awareness of their situation. In Australia, James Cochran, known as Jimmy C, says, "Most of the people I paint are based on real people. It's interesting because I paint on the street and the people I paint are from the street as well. I paint homeless people a lot. There is something really honest about them. It has something to do with the human struggle. They are in a bad position, and I'm trying to capture their spirit to survive."

4 Two questions **inevitably** arise[3] with regard to street art. First, is it legal? And second, is it "real" art? The answers to these questions lead to a third: Should these paintings be left in place, or should they be removed?

5 Banksy himself recognizes that street artists are working in a "legal gray area." In most cases, street art simply appears in the morning, having been made quickly and secretly under the cover of darkness. If the painting appears on the wall of a privately owned building, the owner of the building may choose to keep it or remove it. In some cases, the wall may even be taken down and sold to an art dealer. The owner of the Welsh garage where Banksy painted *Season's Greetings* is thought to have made a significant amount of money by selling his garage walls.

6 Art created on publicly owned property, however, is a different matter. Stephen Yarwood, former mayor of Adelaide, Australia, welcomed street art, saying, "Art isn't just for art galleries . . . Cities are the best art galleries you could possibly have." This is, however, not a common opinion. When Banksy painted inside a London subway train, his

---

[1]**pledge allegiance** (v phr) to promise to be loyal, often to a country symbolized by a flag
[2]**marginalized** (adj) having a less important position in society
[3]**arise** (v) to come up

work was quickly cleaned away because it violated Transport for London's strict anti-graffiti **policy**. There is no universal distinction between art and graffiti, as appreciation for art depends on individual opinion. As such, while Banksy's works are highly regarded[4] today, works by his less famous colleagues are often removed, and their creators are sometimes arrested for **vandalism**.

7   It seems, however, that the popularity of Banksy may be leading to a new **acceptance** of street painting as a true art form. Jimmy C has seen a change in attitude in the years that he has been painting outdoors. He says, "I've met police, security guards that were 10 years ago chasing graffiti artists and now they're buying canvases of graffiti or street art books for their coffee table." Banksy is thought to be a multimillionaire, his money coming from private works for **affluent** art collectors and from books of **reproductions** of his street paintings. American artist Shepard Fairey's street paintings have drawn attention to many issues, including hunger, racism, and diabetes. He now has works in the Museum of Modern Art in New York City and the Victoria and Albert Museum in London. London street artist Ben Eine, who in his youth was arrested over 20 times for painting on buildings, had a painting hanging in the White House.

8   Indeed, Banksy's own work has achieved a level of public recognition that he may not have anticipated when he first started spray-painting walls in the 1990s. In 2020, a Banksy painting was unveiled on the wall of a hospital in Southampton, England, in full collaboration with hospital management. The painting shows a young boy playing with a new toy. He has discarded his comic book superhero toys in a garbage can. Instead, he is making a different kind of superhero fly through the air: a nurse wearing a uniform and face mask.

---

[4]**highly regarded** (adj phr) valued; prized

B MAIN IDEAS Answer the questions.

1. Which statement best summarizes the reading?

    a. Banksy is the most prominent street artist in the world, but his identity is a mystery.

    b. Street art is nothing more than common vandalism; these painters should be arrested.

    c. Street artists are gaining more acceptance for their talents and their messages about society.

2. How does the author view street artists?

    a. They are people who care about social issues and want to share their concerns.

    b. They are uneducated people who probably wrote on their desks at school.

    c. They are talented artists who cannot afford a real art studio or equipment.

C DETAILS Complete with information from the passage.

1. Write the name of a painting that does the following.

   a. Encourages people to be creative: _____

   b. Warns people about pollution: _____

   c. Expresses concerns about consumerism: _____

2. Complete the sentences.

   a. Blek le Rat paints marginalized people on the sides of buildings because he wants to _____ of their situation.

   b. By painting homeless people, Jimmy C is trying to capture

   _____.

   c. It is often unclear whether or not street art is legal. Banksy calls this a "legal _____."

   d. While Banksy's works are highly regarded today, those of his less famous colleagues are often _____. These less famous painters are sometimes even _____.

3. Write the name of the painter each statement applies to.

   a. He is probably a multimillionaire: _____

   b. Some of his paintings draw attention to diabetes: _____

   c. One of his paintings hung in the White House: _____

D DETAILS The identity of Banksy is a secret. What can you infer about him? Write Yes or No. Then share your answers and reasoning with a partner.

1. _____ He knows a lot about the world's problems.

2. _____ He studied art at college or university.

3. _____ He is single and has no children.

4. _____ He enjoys working by himself.

5. _____ He is a skilled businessperson.

REFLECT Take a position on street art.

You are on a committee to make your town more beautiful. Discuss the questions in a group.

1. Consider Stephen Yarwood's statement: "Art isn't just for art galleries . . . Cities are the best art galleries you could possibly have." Do you agree? Should your town allow street art? Explain.

2. When street art is created, how would you determine what is permitted and what should be removed? In other words, who makes the decision, and what is it based on?

WRITE

You are going to write a review of a painting, a novel, a movie, or any other creative work. In your review, you will both *explain* the work (show what it is about) and *critique* it (show why you think it has value and/or what you think is lacking in the work). Use the ideas, vocabulary, and skills from the unit.

A MODEL Read the essay. Look at the painting and decide whether you agree with the review.

Review of *The Boat* by Ted Harrison

1   *The Boat* is a painting by British Canadian artist Ted Harrison (1926–2015). Ted Harrison was a former art teacher who lived in Malaysia and New Zealand before moving to northern Canada in his 40s. At first glance, Ted Harrison's paintings look childish, with bright colors and simple lines. This is his distinct style, which made him famous. However, through his paintings, he

expressed a variety of emotions about life in the far north. In doing so, he painted the north in a way that no other artist has ever done. *The Boat*, painted in 1986, is a classic example of his work.

2   *The Boat* is a simple and colorful painting. The painting shows three people (perhaps a mother, father, and daughter), who have just finished a journey in a small boat, in a remote landscape in northern Canada. They are wearing winter coats, but the women are not wearing hats. With their dark hair, they possibly represent Canada's indigenous population, which is a common theme in Harrison's paintings. The people are walking away from the boat, but Harrison does not show us anything about them. We need to use our imagination to guess who they are and where they are going. The painting is typical of Harrison's style in that the lines are clean and bold, and the colors are unrealistic. The boat is bright orange, and there is a pink sky, a yellow lake, and a purple beach.

3   This painting is appealing in that it is bright and simplistic. Harrison says he was influenced by British artists such as L. S. Lowry and Norman Cornish, who painted everyday scenes of

ordinary people. Harrison did not paint portraits of people in a formal studio. He painted people doing normal things: playing baseball, going on a school field trip, or playing in the snow. People instantly find a personal connection with his paintings, as they remember doing these activities themselves. As an art teacher, Harrison had received formal art training, and he certainly knew how to paint realistic scenes. Despite that, he chose to bring his own style to his work, using bright colors to express joyful emotions.

4   Still, not all of Harrison's paintings express positive emotions. While Harrison is known for his use of bright colors, this often disguises another theme in his paintings: the reality of life in the far north. In *The Boat*, the people are alone on the beach. They have their heads down, and their hair is blowing in the wind, suggesting a feeling of discomfort. On the other side of the water there is a house, which may be the house they have traveled from. There are no other buildings. Harrison is showing the difficulties of living far from others in a very cold climate. There are three black birds on the boat. Harrison's paintings sometimes included black birds, and we can only speculate about whether Harrison intended these to symbolize bad luck or a dark future.

5   Ted Harrison's work clearly shows incredible artistic talent and a unique approach to painting, particularly of a specific landscape. His art is popular with young children, and many are taught how to paint a "Ted Harrison–style" picture at school. But it would be a mistake to dismiss Harrison's paintings as suitable only for elementary school students, as they provide valuable insight into the landscape and lifestyle in this part of the world.

B   ANALYZE THE MODEL Work with a partner to outline the essay.

Title		
Introduction	Background	
	Thesis statement	
First body paragraph: Description	Topic sentence	
	Supporting ideas/Details	
Second body paragraph: Analysis	Topic sentence	
	Supporting ideas/Details	
Third body paragraph: Analysis	Topic sentence	
	Supporting ideas/Details	
Conclusion	Concluding opinion	
	Final thought	

WRITING SKILL   Write a review

In a review of a piece of art, you should do two things: (a) describe or summarize the work of art, and (b) give your critical opinion of it. Your description of the work should be no more than one-third of the essay; the rest should be your analysis.

In your analysis, some questions you may want to address are:

- ➤ Why was the work created? What was the artist trying to achieve?
- ➤ How successful was the artist in achieving his or her goals?
- ➤ What are the strengths of the work? What are its weaknesses?
- ➤ Does the work remind you of anything else, or is it unique?
- ➤ Who might enjoy this work?

When you write your review, remember these important points:

1. You can look up some background details, such as dates and places, but you don't need to do a lot of research since you are mostly giving your opinion.
2. Your review can focus on the positive or negative aspects of the work. There are no right or wrong opinions; just be sure you support your points.
3. Your review should explain why you have a certain reaction to the work. Use expressions such as:

   - ▸ *The artist succeeds (does not succeed) in . . . because . . .*

   - ▸ *The artist accomplishes (doesn't accomplish) his or her goal of . . . because . . .*

   - ▸ *The work is (not) effective in . . . because . . .*

   - ▸ *The work would (not) appeal to . . . because . . .*

C APPLY Choose one of the street paintings in the reading, *Making a Statement, One Wall at a Time.* Complete the sentences with your own thoughts, changing words as appropriate.

1. The artist succeeds (does not succeed) in _____

   because _____

2. The artist accomplishes (doesn't accomplish) his goal of

   _____ because _____

   _____

3. The work is (not) effective in _____

   because _____

4. The work would (not) appeal to _____

   because _____

D NOTICE THE GRAMMAR Find the following sentences in the readings. With a partner, discuss the meaning of the word *this* in each sentence.

1. Also missing at Lascaux are paintings of trees, flowers, and other plants. We can only speculate about what this means . . . (Reading 1, par. 3)

2. Instead, the same signs repeat across different people, locations, and time periods. This suggests that the shapes had a meaning beyond just decoration. (Reading 1, par. 7)

3. While Harrison is known for his use of bright colors, this often disguises another theme in his paintings: the reality of life in the far north. (Model, par. 4)

GRAMMAR   The pronoun *this*

You already know pronouns such as *he*, *she*, or *it* are used to refer to a person or thing that has already been mentioned. The pronoun *this* can be used to refer to an idea, or even an entire sentence, that comes before it. Use *this* to connect and develop ideas from sentence to sentence without repeating a lot of words. In these examples, the pronoun *this* is in bold and the noun phrase or idea it refers to is underlined.

> *Marcel Ravidat discovered the Lascaux caves.* **This** *was a huge event in archaeology.* (**This** refers to the discovery of the Lascaux caves.)

> *Banksy is respected, while his colleagues are often arrested.* **This** *seems very unfair.*

> *At first glance, Ted Harrison's paintings look childish, with bright colors and simple lines.* **This** *is his distinct style, which made him famous.*

Use *it* when you are referring to a single item. Use *this* when you are referring to an idea, an action, or a statement.

> The Boat *was painted by Ted Harrison.* **It** *shows a northern landscape.*

> The Boat *has bright colors and clean lines.* **This** *is typical of Harrison's style.*

Sometimes, it is not clear what *this* refers to. In this case, it's best to avoid *this* and use more specific words.

> Original: *Banksy's latest piece of art was shown on TV last night;* **this** *shocked viewers.*
> (What shocked viewers? Banksy's art or that it was shown on TV?)

> Revision: *Banksy's latest piece of art was shown on TV last night. The images shocked viewers.*

E GRAMMAR Underline what *this* refers to in each sentence.

1. Over 100 million copies of *The Little Prince* have been sold. **This** makes it one of the best-selling books of all time.

2. Artist Paul Gauguin moved to the island of Tahiti in 1891. **This** marked a turning point in his career.

3. Leonardo da Vinci's *Mona Lisa* is one of the most famous women in the world—but who was she? **This** is the big question.

4. I saw a message that said any concert tickets not sold by Friday will be reduced to half price. **This** is a huge bargain!

5. I heard the cleaners removed another painting from the wall of the railway station yesterday. **This** is such a waste of time!

F GRAMMAR Complete the sentences with *this* or *it*.

1. Anish Kapoor's sculpture *Cloud Gate*, located in Chicago, is made of 168 steel plates. _____ is commonly known as "The Bean."

2. Some of the best-selling books in the world are about weight loss. Does _____ surprise you?

3. Ben left school to become a painter. _____ was a huge disappointment to his parents.

4. *The Scream* was painted in 1893 by Edvard Munch. _____ shows the distorted figure of a person standing on a bridge.

5. The music played in the film is amazing! _____ was composed by Beethoven.

6. Mexican artist Frida Kahlo suffered from severe pain as a result of an accident. _____ is a common theme in her paintings.

G EDIT Read the paragraph. Find and correct five errors with *it* or *this*.

What is the blackest paint in the world? In 2014, Surrey NanoSystems developed a very deep shade of black, called Vantablack, for use by aerospace engineers. This new shade caught the attention of artists. One of them was Anish Kapoor, a sculptor known for creating giant objects in public places. Kapoor signed a contract with Surrey NanoSystems, giving him the exclusive rights to use Vantablack. It angered other artists, who also wanted to use Vantablack. One of them was painter Stuart Semple, who had created his own pink color. Semple decided to sell his pink paint on his website, with a message saying that anyone connected to Kapoor could not buy this. It caused a huge reaction, and Semple sold 5,000 jars of pink paint. But it was not the end of the story. Semple also decided to create his own very dark black. Working with chemists, he created Black 1.0. He sent 1,000 samples to artists around the world and received positive feedback. It was encouraging to Semple, who moved on to Black 2.0 and Black 3.0, widely considered to be darker than Vantablack. Semple's Black 3.0 is available online to artists all over the world—but not to Anish Kapoor.

PLAN & WRITE

H BRAINSTORM In a small group, think about a creative work that you might want to review: a painting, photograph, book, movie, or piece of music. Complete the table with some initial thoughts. Then choose the topic you have the best ideas for.

Name of work	Details: artist/author/ filmmaker; date; place	Description: key details	Critique: key points

I OUTLINE Complete the outline.

Introduction

What is the name of the work? _____

What basic information should you give? Who made it? When? Where? Why?

_____

What point do you want to make about the work (your thesis)?

_____

Body paragraph 1: Summary

Topic sentence: What is the work about? _____

Supporting ideas/Details: What does it look like, or what story does it tell?

_____

Body paragraph 2: Analysis

Topic sentence: What main point do you want to make about the work?

_____

Supporting ideas/Details: _____

Body paragraph 3: Analysis

Topic sentence: What other main point do you want to make about the work?

_____

Supporting ideas/Details: _____

Conclusion

Summary or concluding opinion: _____

Final thought: _____

One of the most frequently asked questions in academic writing is, "Can I use the first person?" Is it appropriate to say, "I think this painting is . . ."? It depends on certain things:

a. Your subject area. In some areas, such as the social sciences, the first person is more acceptable. In the sciences, the first person is still often avoided.

b. The type of writing you are doing. In a review, your own opinion is important, so you may occasionally use "I think . . .". In an essay describing how something was built, your own position is less important as you are focusing on the construction of a specific structure.

J FIRST DRAFT Use your outline to write a first draft of your review.

K REVISE Use this list as you write your second draft.

- ☐ Did you include a thesis statement? Does everything in your essay relate to it?
- ☐ Did you organize your information in a logical order, with clear paragraphs?
- ☐ Did you cover one main idea in each paragraph?
- ☐ Did you summarize or describe the work?
- ☐ Did you provide a critical analysis of the work?
- ☐ Did you explain why you react in a certain way?
- ☐ Did you end with a clear concluding opinion?

L EDIT Use this list as you write your final draft.

- ☐ Did you use a variety of adjectives and phrases to describe the work in detail?
- ☐ Did you connect ideas between sentences with *this* where appropriate?
- ☐ Did you use other ways to connect the ideas between sentences?

M FINAL DRAFT Reread your essay, expand on any unclear ideas, and correct any errors. Then submit it to your teacher.

REFLECT

A Check (✓) the Reflect activities you can do and the academic skills you can use.

☐ consider the value of art from the past

☐ discuss issues around studying early art

☐ form an opinion about modern street painting

☐ take a position on street art

☐ write a review of a creative work

☐ distinguish facts from opinions

☐ write a review

☐ the pronoun *this*

☐ evaluate evidence for theories

B Write the vocabulary words from the unit in the correct column. Add any other words that you learned. Circle words you still need to practice.

NOUN	VERB	ADJECTIVE	ADVERB & OTHER

C Reflect on the ideas in the unit as you answer these questions.

1. What was the most interesting thing you learned in the unit?

2. Did any of the ideas you read or discussed change your views of painting on city walls? Explain.

3. What artist or art from the unit do you want to learn more about?

Students from Finland pretend to drive bumper cars in an abandoned amusement park near Chernobyl, Ukraine.

CONNECT TO THE TOPIC

1. Why might these students choose to visit this place?

2. What can we learn from exploring places that have been abandoned?

WATCH

GHOST TOWN
AT THE EDGE OF THE WORLD

Pyramiden, an abandoned Russian coal mining settlement

A Watch a video about a remote town and a tour guide who lives there. Write five or six words or phrases you would use to describe Pyramiden. ▶ 6.1

_____

_____

_____

B Watch the video again. Complete the paragraph. ▶ 6.1

Sitting far above the Arctic Circle, Pyramiden is now part of Norway, but it was once a
¹_____ settlement. Sasha first heard about Pyramiden in ²_____
school. Since moving there he has learned a lot about the history of the town. Pyramiden used to be
a main producer of ³_____. Workers were happy to be sent to Pyramiden, and at
its peak, the community was home to 1,000 miners and their families. Many of them say that their
years in Pyramiden were the ⁴_____ years of their lives. Pyramiden's life came to
an end in ⁵_____ when the mine was closed. Today, six permanent residents of the
town give guided tours to a small number of tourists.

C Why do you think Sasha was attracted to Pyramiden? Would *you* like to go there? Explain.

PREPARE TO READ

A VOCABULARY Complete the sentences with the correct form of the words.

commodity (n)	diagnose (v)	hazard (n)	sanctuary (n)	uninhabited (adj)
decline (n)	harsh (adj)	prosperous (adj)	setback (n)	vegetation (n)

1. When you visit the mountains, watch out for natural _____, such as sudden snowstorms and hungry bears.

2. The Amazon region is known for its diverse _____; there are over 750 varieties of trees and 1,500 other plants.

3. Many islands are _____ because it is too expensive or inconvenient to live there.

4. The company had a _____ year, so they gave their employees bonuses.

5. After the new airport was built, the area around the old airport fell into _____, and nearby hotels and restaurants were closed.

6. Victoria experienced some _____ while following her dream to open a restaurant. She couldn't find a suitable site, and she ran out of money, but she didn't give up.

7. People who live in Arctic regions are used to very _____ conditions, with extremely cold temperatures and little daylight during the winter months.

8. Oil is a valuable _____, and many oil-producing countries have become wealthy.

9. Some diseases are difficult to _____ based on symptoms. Special tests are needed to confirm them.

10. Laura donated money to a wildlife _____, where animals are cared for.

B PERSONALIZE Discuss these questions with a partner.

1. What are some natural **hazards** where you live?
2. What do you think is your country's most valuable **commodity**?
3. Have you ever experienced a **setback** in your studies or career? What did you do?

REFLECT Consider why places are abandoned.

> Before you read about some abandoned places, discuss the questions in a group.
>
> 1. Can you think of any places where people no longer live? What do you know about them?
> 2. How do you think an active, prosperous community can become a ghost town over time?
> 3. If you were to visit a ghost town, what would you expect to see? What would you *not* see?

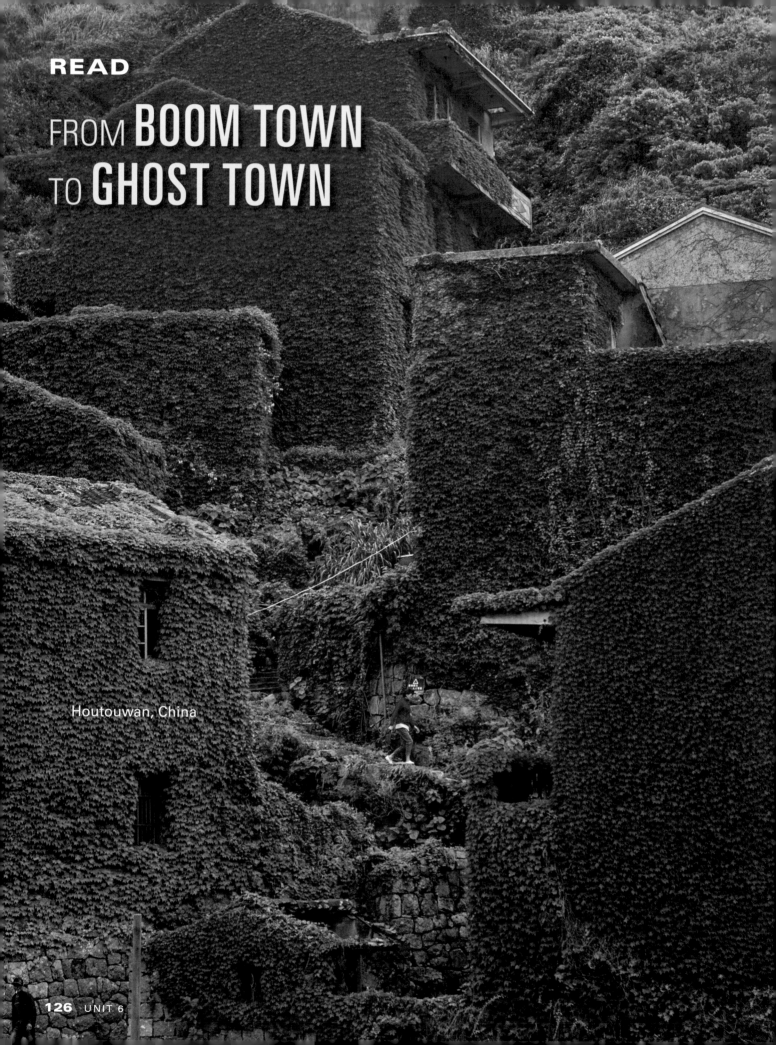

FROM **BOOM TOWN** TO **GHOST TOWN**

Houtouwan, China

🎧 6.1

1   From the Arctic Circle to the seas near Antarctica, the world has many places that were once thriving communities but which are now abandoned. They are known as "ghost towns." An investigation of these places shows us that places are abandoned for many different reasons related to economics, medicine, climate, and more.

Houtouwan, China

2   On China's east coast, Houtouwan was once a **prosperous** fishing village, home to 2,000 fishermen and their families. In the 1990s, however, it became clear that Houtouwan's small harbor was not big enough to accommodate large fishing boats. The villagers started to move to more affluent communities, such as nearby Shanghai, in search of more lucrative employment. Today, every building in the village is covered with a thick, green blanket of **vegetation**, resulting in Houtouwan being called "China's greenest village." Fewer than a dozen people live there today. They make a living selling bottled water to a growing number of tourists, many of whom come on a day trip from Shanghai.

Kolmanskop, Namibia

3   In 1908, a railway worker saw some bright stones shining in the sand of the Namib desert. These turned out to be diamonds, and within a few years, Kolmanskop had become a diamond mining center run by a German mining company. Residents of the town enjoyed a luxurious lifestyle; there were even visits from European theater and opera groups. By the 1930s, however, intensive mining had led to a depletion[1] of diamonds, and with the discovery in 1928 of richer diamond fields south of Kolmanskop, the town fell into **decline**. By 1956, it had been abandoned completely. Today, tourists come to Kolmanskop to see the ruined buildings, many of which are being lost to the desert.

North Brother Island, USA

4   North Brother Island in New York Harbor has had many roles. There are about 25 structures on the island, and in the past, thousands of people called the island home. From the 1880s to World War II, the residents of the island were people with contagious illnesses. After World War II, the island was used by American soldiers and their families. It later became a center for young people who had committed crimes. When the last inhabitants left in 1963, they simply turned out the lights, thinking the island would be used again for another purpose. However, it is now abandoned, except by the many varieties of birds that live there. The island can be seen from downtown New York City, but because it's now a bird **sanctuary**, it is forbidden for tourists to visit.

---

[1]**depletion** (n) a reduction in the amount of something, such as a natural resource

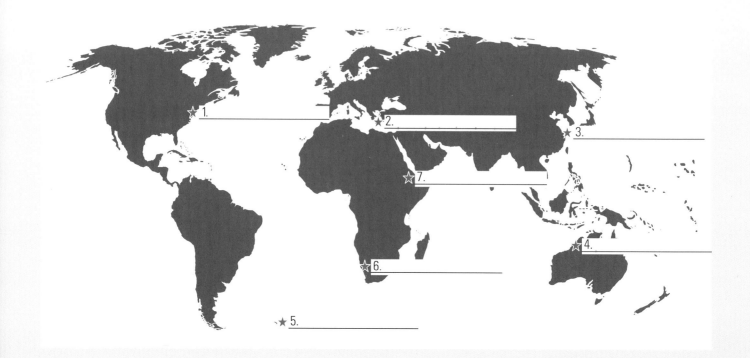

Grytviken, South Georgia

5   In the first half of the 20th century, whales were hunted for the oil that could be made from their fat. Whale oil was a precious **commodity** as it was burned in fuel lamps and made into soap and cosmetics. Grytviken was once the busiest whaling station on South Georgia. At its peak, 500 men lived in Grytviken during the summer months. The station developed into a lively town with a store, movie theater, and post office. After whale populations became depleted and new sources of oil were found, Grytviken closed down in 1966. Today, the community is home only to seals and penguins. The only way to reach Grytviken is by cruise ship; it is a popular stop on the way to Antarctica. The old whaling station remains, as do the wrecks of whaling ships. Many whale bones still lie on the beach.

Cossack, Australia

6   Located in Western Australia, Cossack was the birthplace of the region's pearl[2] industry. From 1866 to 1886, divers harvested pearl shell from the deep seas around Cossack; this was sent to Europe, where it was used to produce buttons for clothes and various decorative items. The divers were primarily Aboriginal Australians, prisoners, and immigrants from Malaysia, Japan, and China. **Hazards** associated with the job included shark attacks, bad weather, and accidents. In 1886, as a result of the depletion of pearls in the Cossack area, the pearl industry moved to the nearby town of Broome. Cossack could not overcome this **setback** and fell into decline. It was abandoned completely in the 1950s. Today, Cossack's buildings are well maintained to attract tourists interested in seeing a small town frozen in the 1950s.

---

[2]**pearl** (n) a white ball formed inside some shellfish that is used in jewelry

Dallol, Ethiopia

7 With an average annual temperature of 95 degrees Fahrenheit (35 degrees Celsius), Dallol is recognized as the hottest place on Earth. Well below sea level, it is also one of the most remote places on Earth. The landscape resembles another planet, with bubbling, green pools of acid[3] and frequent earthquakes and volcanic activity. Yet in the first part of the 20th century, this environment was a center for salt mining. British, Italian, and American companies had economic interests in the area, but the extreme climate made life **harsh**, and so they abandoned their interests. Today, salt is still mined by the local Afar people, but the town of Dallol has been reduced to a few ruined buildings.

Spinalonga, Greece

8 The small Greek island of Spinalonga is a beautiful place with an unpleasant history. From 1903 to 1957, Spinalonga was home to up to 400 residents, all victims of a terrible disease called leprosy. Leprosy damages the nervous system, skin, and eyes; people with the disease often lose the ability to use parts of their body. People **diagnosed** with leprosy were sent to Spinalonga, where they lived with other lepers and received medical care from a doctor who visited once a week. After the development of effective treatments for leprosy, the island closed. It remains **uninhabited**, but many tourists who are fascinated by Spinalonga's history visit the island on day trips by boat from vacation resort towns.

9 As the world changes, the places people choose to live also change. Once-booming towns are abandoned, and new population centers appear. What will be the next place to disappear from the map?

---

[3]**acid** (n) a sour substance, such as lemon juice or vinegar

B MAIN IDEAS Do the tasks.

1. Match each sentence with the place it describes. Use each place only once.

   a. _____ Your great-grandmother's pearl necklace might have come from here.

   b. _____ A lucky find led to the development of a luxury desert community.

   c. _____ If you like the heat, you might like this town.

   d. _____ Modern medicine has made this place unnecessary.

   e. _____ This might be the quietest place in New York City.

   f. _____ This fishing village is now better known for its plant life.

   g. _____ Come here to see penguins and the remains of an old way of life.

2. Which of the following is **not** mentioned as a reason for the decline of a place?

   a. Loss of resources   c. Harsh weather conditions

   b. War   d. Advances in medicine

C DETAILS Complete the table with details about each of the ghost towns in the reading.

Place	Location/ description	Use/economic activity	Reason for decline	What is it like today?
Houtouwan				
Kolmanskop				
North Brother Island				
Grytviken				
Cossack				
Dallol				
Spinalonga				

READING SKILL Synthesize information

The word *synthesize* means "combine," or "bring together." When you synthesize information, you take information from different sources and use it to support a single point. As you read different source materials, look for similarities and differences in the information.

The table in activity C shows that some ghost towns have unique features and also features in common. These include the location of each place, the reason for its growth and decline, and its status today.

If you want to make the point that ghost towns often have extreme climates, you could refer to Grytviken and Dallol. If you want to say that ghost towns disappeared for different reasons, you might refer to Houtouwan, Kolmanskop, and Spinalonga.

D APPLY Imagine you are writing an essay on the reasons ghost towns come into existence. One of your body paragraphs has the topic sentence below. Which details from *From Boom Town to Ghost Town* will be useful to include as examples? Complete the table.

Topic sentence	The depletion of natural resources often causes a town or community to be abandoned.
Supporting ideas/Details	
Concluding sentence	

Kolmanskop, Namibia

WRITING TIP

As you write, you will often need to choose between single-word verbs and phrasal verbs.

Resources were depleted./Resources ran out.

The population declined./The population went down.

The landscape resembles the moon./The landscape looks like the moon.

Some phrasal verbs are more commonly used in informal conversation, not in academic and professional writing. Before choosing a phrasal verb over a single-word verb, make sure it is suitable for what you are writing.

REFLECT Explore the potential of a ghost town.

Discuss the questions in a small group.

1. Which of the abandoned places in the reading would you most like to visit? Why?

2. Do you think the place you have chosen has the potential to develop its tourist industry more? What would be needed? What might discourage tourists from visiting?

PREPARE TO READ

A VOCABULARY Use the correct form of one of the words below to replace the underlined word or phrase in each sentence.

clarity (n)	dominant (adj)	intellectual (adj)	layout (n)	ritual (n)
collapse (n)	drought (n)	laser (n)	revenue (n)	transmit (v)

1. _____ The tea ceremony is a <u>significant ceremonial event</u> at traditional Chinese weddings.

2. _____ As a result of the <u>severe lack of rainfall</u>, the harvest was very poor.

3. _____ Email allows us to <u>send</u> messages more quickly than ever before.

4. _____ The <u>placement</u> of buildings on this college campus is not convenient; for example, the library is too far from the residential buildings.

5. _____ Many medical procedures today are carried out with the use of <u>beams of light</u>; for example, eye surgeons use these to help people with weak vision.

6. _____ Much of the country's <u>income</u> comes from oil.

7. _____ The game of chess is <u>known to require mental ability</u>; good chess players are considered to be very smart.

8. _____ The <u>dramatic fall</u> of the stock market in the 1920s had disastrous effects for many people.

9. _____ <u>The quality of being easily understood</u> is often missing in legal documents.

10. _____ Japan is one of the world's <u>leading</u> economic powers.

B PERSONALIZE Discuss the questions with a partner.

1. Do you enjoy **intellectual** games, such as chess? Explain.

2. If you could change something about the **layout** of your town or city, what would you change?

3. What **rituals** do you follow in your household or in your family? Which is your favorite?

REFLECT Assess your knowledge of your country's history.

Before you read about using technology to find lost civilizations, discuss these questions in a group.

1. What is the most interesting period in your country's history?

2. What lessons can be learned from studying this period?

3. How do you think technology can help us to understand more about the past?

LIDAR

La Carmelita, a Maya site in Tabasco, Mexico, discovered using LiDAR

A PREVIEW Look at the diagram on the next page and skim paragraph 3. Answer the questions.

1. What does LiDAR stand for?

2. How is it useful in investigating lost civilizations?

6.2 *Sometimes, not just towns but entire civilizations disappear. Technology is helping researchers find them.*

1 The Mayan civilization, along with the Aztec and Inca, was one of the **dominant** civilizations of the Americas before the arrival of Europeans in the 16th century. The Maya lived in what is now Mexico and Central America; the civilization was at its peak from AD 250 to AD 900. The Maya built impressive stone structures, including the pyramids[1] for which they are well known, and they grew crops, primarily corn. They made advancements in mathematics, they had a system of writing, and they invented a calendar based on the sun. The Mayan civilization fell into decline around AD 900 and rapidly disappeared, for reasons that remain unclear. The **collapse** of the civilization might have been caused by war, by volcanic activity, or by **drought**.

2 Now, researchers are learning more about the Maya through investigations in Mexico and Guatemala. Some surprising finds have been made, which have given us information about this lost civilization. The tool making these discoveries possible is LiDAR.

3 LiDAR stands for Light Detection and Ranging. This technology makes use of **lasers** to create 3-D pictures. LiDAR has many uses, including in map making, weather forecasting, space exploration, and self-driving cars. When used to investigate lost civilizations, LiDAR devices are put on planes, which fly over the region. These devices **transmit** laser beams to the ground below. When the light bounces back, it provides a "high-tech treasure map." The **layout** of the natural and human-made features below—buildings, roads, waterways—appear on the computer screen, even if they are hidden under dense vegetation. As National Geographic Explorer Thomas Garrison says, "You could walk over the top of a major ruin and miss it. But LiDAR picks up the patterns and makes the features pop out with astounding **clarity**."

4 Results have been impressive. At the Aguada Fénix site in Mexico, the use of LiDAR has revealed the full size of a 1.4-kilometer platform, which was made of earth and includes several buildings on top. This platform is now recognized as the oldest and largest structure in the Mayan region—larger than the biggest pyramid in Egypt. It is thought to have been built 3,000 years ago, long before the peak of the Mayan civilization. Researcher Takeshi Inomata has calculated that it must have taken 5,000 people more than 6 years to build it. Inomata believes the structure might have been used for ceremonies, "a place of gathering, possibly involving processions and other **rituals** we can only imagine." This is supported by the discovery of a network of roads leading to the site.

5 Since no houses have been found near the structure, researchers conclude that users of the site might not have lived nearby. However, the large size of the structure suggests that the Maya were in the process of leaving their hunter-gatherer way of life at the time of construction. Perhaps this was the foundation for a large city with more permanent homes. The size of the structure also suggests the ability of different people to collaborate on a project. Researcher Verónica Vázquez López has noticed that some of the layers of soil used to build the platform were laid down in a systematic pattern of different soil colors. These may have symbolized the contribution of different groups to the building project.

6 Equally interesting discoveries have been made in Guatemala. The PACUNAM LiDAR Initiative, a survey from the air of 2,100 square kilometers, has shown the ruins of a civilization that was more complex and advanced than previously believed. As Thomas Garrison, one of the researchers on the PACUNAM project, says, "It's almost like we're looking at them for the first time again."

7 One of the largest investigation sites in Guatemala is the ancient city of Tikal. Researchers once believed they had discovered every building in Tikal, but LiDAR revealed otherwise. LiDAR mapping showed that a pyramid-shaped object, previously thought to be a small hill, was actually a building. It may have been a ceremonial structure, and may even have contained the tomb of a king. In the same region, a key development was the discovery of a large fortress[2] between Tikal and nearby El Zotl.

---

[1]**pyramid** (n) a building with a square base and a triangular top

[2]**fortress** (n) a structure built to defend a place in time of conflict

The fortress, known as La Cuernavilla, is one of the largest defensive systems in the Americas; it includes watchtowers, moats[3], and high walls. This is significant, as it suggests that the Mayan people must have lived in fear of attack from enemies.

8   The use of LiDAR to investigate Mayan ruins is not only an **intellectual** pursuit; it also has economic benefits. In Guatemala, the government has been supportive of the use of LiDAR because the Guatemalan tourist industry, a significant source of **revenue** for the country, is largely based on the appeal of ancient ruins. The more ruins LiDAR finds, the more possibilities for tourist attractions. In addition, LiDAR mapping helps in the creation of a database, which keeps records of cultural items. Vandalism and theft are often problems at Mayan sites. LiDAR helps track the damage.

---

[3]**moat** (n) a human-made body of water around a castle or fortress

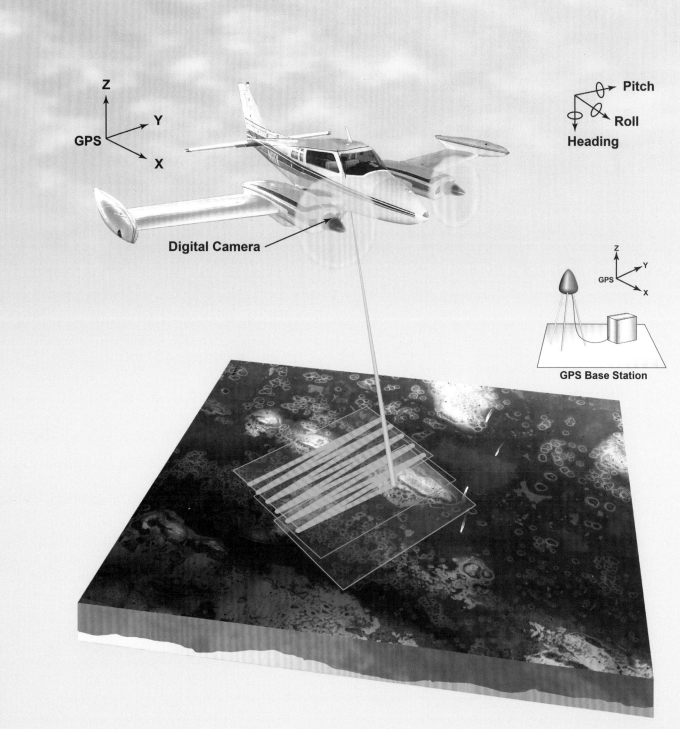

LOST IN TIME **135**

9 However, it is worth keeping in mind that LiDAR is limited in what it can do. It cannot, for example, allow researchers to see below the ground, so tunnels and ruins now covered by earth cannot be seen. Neither does it take away the need for physical labor. National Geographic Explorer Francisco Estrada-Belli says, "We'll still need to dig and hack our way through the jungle." However, the use of LiDAR is making the process much faster and more efficient. As Estrada-Belli says, "Now we have a very accurate map to guide us." There is still much that remains unknown about the Mayan civilization, but LiDAR looks certain to be a useful tool in future investigations. In the words of PACUNAM director Marianne Hernandez, "This is a beginning, a doorway that opens to decades of further research."

B MAIN IDEAS Write the number of the paragraph where these ideas appear.

a. _____ No one is sure why the Mayan civilization fell into decline.

b. _____ A newly discovered Mayan structure is bigger than an Egyptian pyramid.

c. _____ Different groups might have worked together on a building project in Mexico.

d. _____ Researchers found more than they expected at Tikal.

e. _____ LiDAR is a useful tool, but there are some things it cannot do.

C DETAILS Choose the best ending for each sentence.

1. LiDAR is a _____.

    a. kind of plane that flies over ancient ruins and takes photos of them

    b. form of laser technology that shows what lies under vegetation

    c. tool for drawing maps of human-made features, such as roads and waterways

2. Scientists in Mexico have found _____.

    a. a huge platform with buildings on top

    b. a pyramid, similar to ones in Egypt

    c. a collection of houses, built by the Mayan people

3. The use of LiDAR in Guatemala has shown researchers that _____.

    a. the Mayan civilization was older than they had believed

    b. the Maya fought in wars more than previously thought

    c. the Mayan civilization was more developed than previously thought

D DETAILS What do the following words refer to?

1. **This** in the last sentence of paragraph 4

    a. the Aguada Fénix site   b. Takeshi Inomata's theory   c. the structure

2. **These** in the last sentence of paragraph 5

    a. residential buildings   b. permanent settlements   c. soil colors

3. **This** in the last sentence of paragraph 7

    a. the ancient city of Tikal   b. the moat   c. the large defense system

E DETAILS Can the following be inferred from the reading? Write Y for *Yes* or N for *No*.

1. _____ Rituals and ceremonies were important aspects of Mayan civilization.

2. _____ Mayan society was divided into different groups.

3. _____ The Maya were an aggressive, war-loving civilization.

4. _____ There are no modern descendants of the Maya.

CRITICAL THINKING Apply the past to the present

It is often said that learning about history helps us (a) to understand the present, and (b) to make the right decisions in the present. This is true for individuals, for organizations, and for countries. When you read about a historical event, whether positive or negative, try to make a connection between the event and the present. What can be learned from it?

F APPLY Work with a small group. Discuss the questions and take notes on each other's answers. Then discuss how you might synthesize your answers into a larger lesson. Share your ideas with the class.

	Name _____	Name _____	Name _____
What event in your life taught you a valuable lesson? What did you do differently afterward?			
What event in your country's history taught the people a valuable lesson?			
What event in your country's history could people have learned from, but did not? Why not?			

REFLECT Imagine further uses of technology.

Discuss the questions in a small group.

1. In which place in the world would you like to see LiDAR used? What do you think might be discovered?

2. How do you think LiDAR is used in map making, weather forecasting, space exploration, and self-driving cars?

WRITE

UNIT TASK Write a cause-effect essay about an event in history.

You are going to write a short essay focusing on *either* the causes *or* the effects of a historical event that had an impact on the people of your country or a country you know about. Use the ideas, vocabulary, and skills from the unit.

A MODEL Read the essay. Highlight the effects.

Effects of the Dust Bowl Disaster

1   At the beginning of the 20th century, the grasslands of the Midwestern United States, known as the Great Plains, were considered a "land of opportunity." Land was plentiful, and the demand for wheat, corn, and other crops was increasing. However, farmers could not have predicted the environmental disaster that took place in the 1930s in the region. A severe drought combined with the overuse of certain farming techniques led to a series of dust storms, which caused great harm between 1935 and 1938. This event was known as the Dust Bowl. The Dust Bowl was a terrible event, but it eventually led to positive changes for the agriculture of the region.

2   The Dust Bowl storms caused serious environmental and structural damage in the Midwest. Since the top layer of soil had turned to dust and blown away, crops could not grow properly, and harvests were poor. In some places, up to 75 percent of the topsoil was lost. The death rate among animals increased, too, as they breathed in dust. This caused further food shortages. Many buildings lost their roofs and windows because of the winds. The effects of the storms were even felt in cities such as Chicago and Washington; after one particularly strong storm, there were reports of ships in the Atlantic Ocean being covered with dust.

3   Agricultural devastation led to serious problems for the people of the region. They could not keep the dust out of their houses, and many suffered from breathing problems. Dust pneumonia was a common lung condition caused by breathing in dust. In some cases, people who had sealed their doors and windows to keep out the dust died from carbon monoxide poisoning caused by fuel lamps. Government support did not come quickly enough to help farming families, and many were forced to leave their homes. With their possessions packed into trucks, 3.5 million people abandoned the Midwest and traveled west, attracted by the promise of a better life in California. In reality, they ended up in refugee camps where there was not enough food. Many people, especially children, died of starvation.

4   In the long term, however, the Dust Bowl led to improvements in farming techniques and agricultural policy. As the seriousness of the problem became clear, more than 200 million new trees were planted across the Midwest, in an attempt to prevent loss of soil caused by wind. Farmers recognized that they should have been using techniques such as planting a different crop in a field each year to maintain the quality of their soil. These changes meant that by the end of the 1930s, the amount of dust had decreased by 65 percent. In the 1950s, the region experienced another period of drought, but the effects were less severe. It would, however, take the Midwest many years to fully recover from the Dust Bowl.

5   The Dust Bowl was a tragic event in U.S. history and had a significant effect on the lives of many. In 1939, the rain came back and the tragedy passed, but lessons can be learned from the crisis. Climate change around the world has led to drought in many countries. It is important to use appropriate farming techniques designed to reduce the effects of changing weather conditions. Perhaps the most important lesson to be learned from the Dust Bowl disaster is that nature should be respected.

B ANALYZE THE MODEL Work with a partner to outline the essay.

Title		
Introduction	Background	
	Thesis statement	
First body paragraph	Topic sentence	
	Supporting ideas/ Details	
Second body paragraph	Topic sentence	
	Supporting ideas/ Details	
Third body paragraph	Topic sentence	
	Supporting ideas/ Details	
Conclusion	Final thoughts	

WRITING SKILL   Explain causes and effects

When you write about causes, you show why something happened. When you write about effects, you write about the results of the event. Here are some tips to keep in mind:

1. Your thesis statement should briefly state what the causes or effects are. Let your reader know what to expect in your essay.

2. Your paragraphs should each focus on a specific cause or effect. Support your points with statistics or other evidence. For example, don't just tell your reader that many people had to leave their homes; give a number.

3. Say what was learned (or what can be learned) from the event. You can also consider speculating on what *must*, *might*, or *should* have happened.

4. Use language such as:

    ▶ Cause-and-effect phrases

    One of the main reasons for . . . was . . .

    A key result/consequence of . . . was . . .

    ▶ Verb phrases indicating a cause and effect

    The . . . contributed to/led to . . .

    The . . . resulted in/brought about/gave rise to . . .

GRAMMAR   Past modals

Past modals are used to express certainty, possibility, ability, regret, or criticism of an event or situation in the past. They are formed with modal + *have* + past participle of the verb.

If something in the past is **probable**, use *must (not) have.*

*The miners **must have been** disappointed when the mine closed.*

*They **must not have realized** that it would be difficult to find work.*

If something in the past was **possible**, use *might (not)* or *may (not) have.*

*Poor management decisions **might have led** to the decline of the industry.*

*The farmers **may not have understood** the need to rotate their crops.*

To describe a **lack of ability**, use *could not have.*

*They **could not have known** the climate would be so harsh.*

To express a **regret** or a **criticism**, use *should (not) have.*

*The company **should have taken** better care of its employees.*

*The ship's captain **should not have ignored** the weather forecast.*

C GRAMMAR Complete the sentences with a suitable past modal. Use the verb in parentheses. Explain to a partner why you chose each modal.

1. The diamond miners in Kolmanskop _____ (not know) that their town would fall into decline quickly in the 1930s.

2. The families who lived in Pyramiden in the 1980s were happy; they _____ (be) unhappy to leave their home.

3. Stuck on an island in the South Atlantic, workers in Grytviken _____ (feel) lonely sometimes.

4. Anyone who tried to establish a lucrative business in Dallol before visiting the region _____ (not predict) how difficult life would be.

5. Anyone who went to live on Spinalonga after being diagnosed with leprosy _____ (experience) a sense of fear and uncertainty about the future.

6. The people who employed divers in Cossack _____ (protect) the divers from sharks.

A family during the Dust Bowl

D GRAMMAR Look at the following sentences from the model. What inferences can you make? Use any past modal. Be prepared to explain your inference.

1. A severe drought combined with the overuse of certain farming techniques led to a series of dust storms, which caused great harm between 1935 and 1938.

   The people must not have known about proper farming techniques.

2. In some cases, people who had sealed their doors and windows to keep out the dust died from carbon monoxide poisoning caused by fuel lamps.

3. Government support did not come quickly enough to help farming families, and many were forced to leave their homes.

4. With their possessions packed into trucks, 3.5 million people abandoned the Midwest and traveled west, attracted by the promise of a better life in California. In reality, they ended up in refugee camps where there was not enough food.

5. In the 1950s, the region experienced another period of drought, but the effects were less severe.

E EDIT Read the paragraph. Find and correct four errors with the the use of past modals.

Headless Men

Old stories and legends are full of civilizations that may or may not have actually exist. These include a group of female warriors called Amazons, a race of giants called Hyperboreans, and the most extreme of all, a race of headless men, whose faces were on their chests. These headless men appear in Greek and Roman writing on history and are even mentioned in the works of Shakespeare. They were thought to live in India, in Ethiopia, and near the Nile River. Of course, headless men could not existed in reality, so what were they? Modern scientists have two theories. First, they might been gorillas or other large primates. Second, they might have been members of tribes who raised their shoulders and lowered their heads as they walked. No matter what they were, it should have been terrifying to meet someone who appeared to have no head!

WRITING TIP

The use of past modals is one way to hedge your statements. When you hedge, you "soften" your arguments to show that your opinion is not the only answer, and there may be other possibilities. You can also hedge with sentence starters like these:

- It appears that . . .
- It seems likely that . . .
- Evidence suggests that . . .

- There is a possibility that . . .
- A possible/probable outcome was . . .
- Data/Research suggests that . . .

PLAN & WRITE

F BRAINSTORM In a small group, think of two or three historical events. For each one, discuss possible causes and/or effects. Your events could be positive, such as a scientific or medical breakthrough, or the production of a cultural work. They could also be negative, such as a natural disaster or an act of hostility.

Event			
Key details (when, where, who?)			
What caused it?			
What were the results?			
Lessons learned?			

G RESEARCH Consider these ideas as you research an event.

If you are focusing on causes, think about the actions, decisions, or conditions that led to the event. If it was a negative event, could it have been prevented? If you are focusing on effects, think about social, environmental, economic, political, and other effects. What lessons can be learned? Decide whether your essay will emphasize causes or effects.

H OUTLINE Complete the outline.

Introduction

Background _____

Thesis _____

Body paragraph 1

Topic sentence _____

Supporting ideas/Details _____

Body paragraph 2

Topic sentence _____

Supporting ideas/Details _____

Body paragraph 3

Topic sentence _____

Supporting ideas/Details _____

Conclusion

_____

_____

I FIRST DRAFT Use your outline to write a first draft of your essay.

J REVISE Use this list as you write your second draft.

☐ Did you include basic information about your event (e.g., time, place, people involved)?

☐ Did you make it clear whether you are describing primarily causes or effects?

☐ Did you write paragraphs with one specific idea, which is supported with details?

☐ Did you explain the significance of the event?

☐ Did you make assumptions and draw conclusions about the event?

K EDIT Use this list as you write your final draft.

☐ Did you use past modals in your essay to speculate about events?

☐ Are all past participles correct?

☐ Did you use different cause-and-effect phrases?

L FINAL DRAFT Reread your essay, expand on any unclear ideas, and correct any errors. Then submit it to your teacher.

REFLECT

A Check (✓) the Reflect activities you can do and the academic skills you can use.

☐ consider why places are abandoned

☐ explore the potential of a ghost town

☐ assess your knowledge of your country's history

☐ imagine further uses of technology

☐ write a cause-effect essay about an event in history

☐ synthesize information

☐ explain causes and effects

☐ past modals

☐ apply the past to the present

B Write the vocabulary words from the unit in the correct column. Add any other words that you learned. Circle words you still need to practice.

NOUN	VERB	ADJECTIVE	ADVERB & OTHER

C Reflect on the ideas in the unit as you answer these questions.

1. What was the most interesting thing you learned in the unit?

2. Has this unit inspired you to visit any of the places mentioned in the readings? If so, which one(s)?

3. Can you apply anything you have learned in this unit to your own country? Explain why.

Two Emirati friends greet each other in Abu Dhabi, United Arab Emirates.

CONNECT TO THE TOPIC

1. How do you and your friends greet each other? How do you greet people you've never met before?

2. Apart from language, what are other differences in how people from different cultures communicate?

HOW DO YOU PREFER TO COMMUNICATE?

A singing group in Edinburgh, Scotland

A Watch the video and complete the table. ▶ 7.1

	How do they prefer to communicate?	What challenges do they face when using this form of communication?	What would they say to people about this form of communication?
Alishia			
Cate			
Tim			

B PERSONALIZE Discuss these questions with a partner.

1. Which of the three speakers interests you the most?

2. What would you like to ask that person about their method of communication?

PREPARE TO READ

A VOCABULARY Complete the sentences with the correct form of the words.

assign (v)	gender (n)	inherent (adj)	notion (n)	status (n)
controversial (adj)	hypothesis (n)	linguistic (adj)	provoke (v)	superficial (adj)

1. In many societies, people of higher _____ use different words and expressions than people in lower social positions.

2. There are some _____ differences between the articles, but when you read them more closely, you see that they make similar arguments.

3. Many people believe in the _____ that some languages are naturally more beautiful than others. In reality, this idea is not true.

4. In some languages, nouns are masculine or feminine. The _____ of a word is not related to its meaning; for example, in French, a book is masculine, but a table is feminine.

5. Before designing the experiment, the researcher formulated a(n) _____. She predicted that most bilingual speakers communicate in one language at home and the other at work.

6. The human world is known for its _____ diversity—but do you know how many different languages there are?

7. The school's recent tuition increase _____ a strong reaction.

8. What is the best age to learn a new language? That's a(n) _____ topic!

9. The teacher divided the class into teams and _____ a color to each team.

10. A need to communicate with others is _____ in all humans. Children grow up using language naturally without being taught.

B PERSONALIZE Discuss these questions with a partner.

1. Does your first language have **gender**? Is gender in language useful? Explain.

2. Do you think some people have an **inherent** ability to communicate well? To what extent can communication skills be learned?

REFLECT Consider the relationship between language and thought.

Before you read about language and thought, discuss these questions in a small group.

1. Some languages have words that cannot easily be translated. For example, the Inuit language has a word, *iktsuarpok*, which refers to the excitement you feel when someone is coming to your home. Why do you think there is no equivalent word in English?

2. Does your first language have any words that have no equivalent word in English? What does this tell us about the relationship between language, culture, and thought?

THE LANGUAGE-THOUGHT CONNECTION

A PREVIEW Answer the questions.

1. Look at the animals in the photo. What are they called in English?

2. English has a small number of words for these animals, whereas the people who live in this region have many. What can you infer from this difference?

A Dinka herder, Sudan

7.1 *Is there a connection between the language we speak and the way we see the world? Some linguists who study the science and structure of language think so. Others are not so sure.*

1   Imagine you are walking across a flat landscape in East Africa. You come across a large creature that you correctly identify as a cow. You see several more of these creatures, and you **assign** them all the same name: "cow." However, for the Dinka people of Sudan, cows are fundamental to their economic and cultural lives. Cows are traditionally used to produce food, medicine, and clothing; they are a sign of wealth and are used as a form of payment. It is no surprise, then, that the Dinka have over 400 words to describe the varieties, colors, actions, and diseases of cows.

2   Many miles away, in the Solomon Islands in the South Pacific, where coconuts are a key commodity, locals have nine different words for "coconut." Do the Solomon Islanders view coconuts differently because they have more words to describe them? Do the Dinka of Sudan see differences in cows not noticeable to those who do not speak their language? In short, what is the relationship between **linguistic** differences and thought processes?

3   This was the question asked in the 1930s and 1940s by linguists Edward Sapir and Benjamin Lee Whorf. The resulting theory, the Sapir-Whorf **hypothesis**, suggests that an individual's view of the world is determined or influenced by the language that the individual speaks. Language is not simply a list of grammar rules or vocabulary items; it plays a key role in how we process and interpret experiences and information.

4   Let's look at a few examples. Some languages do not use terms such as "left" and "right" when describing location or giving directions. They use the directions found on a compass[1]. A speaker of Guugu Yimithirr, a minority language spoken in Australia, would not give directions to his house by telling you to turn right. He would also not say that he has hurt his left leg. Instead, he might tell you to "travel north-west" to visit him, and he might refer to the injured limb as his "south-south-east leg." Frequent use of this type of phrasing has benefits. Speakers of Guugu Yimithirr have been shown to have a much stronger sense of direction than speakers of languages that do not describe direction in this way.

---

[1]**compass** (n) a small tool that shows direction: north, south, east, and west

5 Psychologist Lera Boroditsky has explored the influence of **gender** on the words used to describe objects. In many languages, everyday objects such as tables, chairs, pens, and pencils can be masculine or feminine. Boroditsky asked speakers of German and Spanish to describe a bridge. The word "bridge" is feminine in German (*die Brücke*), while in Spanish, it is masculine (*el puente*). The German speakers in the study described the bridge with adjectives that are commonly used to describe females, such as "beautiful" and "elegant," while the Spanish speakers used adjectives often used to describe males, such as "strong" and "powerful." Boroditsky found similar results when participants were asked to describe other everyday objects. Her study suggests that the grammatical gender of an object influences how that object is seen.

6 While the Sapir-Whorf hypothesis has received a lot of attention, it is not accepted as truth by all linguists; in fact, it is **controversial**. Many linguists argue that differences such as the number of words for coconuts or cows are only **superficial** and do not play a significant role in shaping thought processes. Cultures create words to respond to needs, and speakers of different languages simply have different needs. To them, these differences in grammar and vocabulary do not prove that language alone controls a whole culture's thoughts.

7 Another concern is that relating cognitive processing to language differences is problematic: Could the hypothesis be a form of **inherent** discrimination, an outdated **notion**? Specifically, does this theory assume that speakers of certain languages are incapable of certain thoughts? In Whorf's early writings, for example, he described how the Hopi people of the southwestern United States did not express verb tenses in the same way as English speakers. This should in no way suggest an inability to understand time among the Hopi.

8 Today, the "strong" version of the hypothesis, that language *determines* how we see the world, has few followers. There is, however, still support for the "weak" version, that language *influences* worldview. There are several implications of this. Let's think about two key questions.

9 Firstly, do bilingual or multilingual people see the world differently depending on which language they are speaking? In a study of over 1,000 bilingual individuals, over two-thirds reported feeling "like a different person" when changing languages. Think about someone who is bilingual in English and Korean. Korean has a complex system of levels of politeness and formality: The language forms a Korean speaker uses will change according to the age or **status** of the listener.

There are nine different words for "coconut" in the Solomon Islands.

Bilingual speakers need to be more aware of the age and status of the listener when speaking Korean than when speaking English.

10   Secondly, what is the implication of the Sapir-Whorf hypothesis for the world's minority languages? There are around 6,500 languages in the world, and almost half of them are in danger of disappearing. If language is more than a system of sounds, words, and structures, and if we acknowledge its connection to the worldview of its speakers, this means that when a language is lost, we lose more than just a set of grammar and vocabulary. We potentially lose a way of looking at the world that is unique to speakers of that language. This point of view is shared by many linguists, who are working to preserve minority languages.

11   As you have seen, a language is much more than a system of sounds, words, and grammatical structures. It affects how speakers see and interpret the world. This is a controversial topic that **provokes** strong reactions, but it is one that offers rich potential for further research and discussion.

B MAIN IDEAS Choose the correct answers.

1. What is the main idea of this article?

   a. Some languages are more complex and have richer vocabularies than others.

   b. Languages around the world have different systems of grammar.

   c. The way we think is dependent on the structure of our language.

   d. More research is needed to fully understand how language influences the way people see the world.

2. What is the current status of the Sapir-Whorf hypothesis?

   a. No one is currently researching this topic; interest in it died out in the 1930s and 1940s.

   b. It is considered interesting, but many linguists are not convinced about it.

   c. The Sapir-Whorf hypothesis has been shown to be incorrect; no one takes it seriously.

   d. The Sapir-Whorf hypothesis is considered valuable as it explains much about cognition.

C DETAILS Choose the correct ending for each sentence.

1. _____ The Dinka . . .
2. _____ Edward Sapir and Benjamin Lee Whorf . . .
3. _____ Speakers of languages that have gender . . .
4. _____ Critics of the Sapir-Whorf hypothesis . . .
5. _____ Bilingual and multilingual people . . .
6. _____ The world's minority languages . . .

a. should be protected, as they provide insight into the unique way of thinking of their speakers.

b. sometimes say that they feel like two different people when speaking different languages.

c. are concerned that relating language to cognitive processes can lead to false assumptions.

d. see differences between cows that are not usually noticed by casual observers.

e. suggested there might be a relationship between language and thought.

f. might view masculine and feminine nouns differently.

D DETAILS What can you infer from the article? Write Y for *Yes* or N for *No*. Explain your answers to a partner.

1. _____ People whose lives depend on animals or plants often have more words for them.

2. _____ If an English speaker asks a speaker of Guugu Yimithirr for directions, the response might be confusing.

3. _____ German bridges are more beautiful than Spanish bridges.

4. _____ The role played by gender in a language may be more than just grammatical.

5. _____ Koreans are not concerned about the age of a person they meet.

6. _____ It is important to protect the endangered languages of the world.

READING SKILL Annotate a text

As you saw in Unit 1, you need to be an active reader. You need to react to the text, not just passively get information from it. One way to do this is to read with a pen in your hand. As you read, annotate the text. (If you don't want to write in your book, you can also take notes on a separate piece of paper.) Specifically, each time you read a key detail, write a comment, such as an example to illustrate it, or your reaction to it. This serves three purposes:

▸ It allows you to check that you have understood the main ideas of the reading.
▸ It allows you to go beyond what is written in the text and to apply it to other situations you have heard about.
▸ It helps you review the text before a quiz or test.

E APPLY Read the statements from the reading and the sample questions. Then think of your own experiences and make annotations that respond to the questions.

Statement	Your annotation
It is no surprise, then, that the Dinka have over 400 words to describe the varieties, colors, actions, and diseases of cows. (par. 1) (What aspect of life in my culture has a lot of words to describe it?)	*Similar to . . .*
Cultures create words to respond to needs, and speakers of different languages simply have different needs. (par. 6) (Which new words have appeared in my first language in the last 20 years? Why?)	
In a study of over 1,000 bilingual individuals, over two-thirds reported feeling "like a different person" when changing languages. (par. 9) (Do I ever feel this way? When?)	
There are around 6,500 languages in the world, and almost half of them are in danger of disappearing. (par. 10) (Which minority languages in my country are in danger of disappearing? What would be lost if these languages were lost?)	

LEARNING TIP

As you develop your vocabulary, be aware of 'false friends.' These are words that look the same as a word in your first language but that have a different meaning. For example, Spanish speakers must learn that the English word *realize* does not mean *to do* or *to perform*; it means *to understand*.

REFLECT   Evaluate ideas about language and thought.

In your notebook, respond to each of the following statements. Then, in a small group, share your responses and decide which one you all agree or disagree with most.

▶ Bilingual and multilingual people see the world differently depending on which language they are speaking.
▶ It is wrong to say that certain people cannot formulate a specific idea just because their language does not currently have a single word for it.

PREPARE TO READ

A VOCABULARY Choose the word or phrase that shows the meaning of the word in bold.

1. In your culture, is it important to have respect for **authority**?

   a. people with power   b. people with money

2. Is it important in your culture to follow established **conventions**?

   a. ways of acting   b. meetings

3. Since she grew up in poverty, Emily has **empathy** for people in difficult circumstances.

   a. a disconnection from   b. an understanding of the feelings of

4. It is illegal to park on First Street, but the law is rarely **enforced**.

   a. acted upon   b. ignored

5. It is dangerous to **generalize** about people from different cultures.

   a. make big assumptions   b. learn everything

6. When someone is arrested, are the police **inclined to** believe the suspect's story?

   a. likely to   b. reluctant to

7. In his presentation, Jack gave an **overview** of the findings of his research project.

   a. the main points   b. the details

8. Do all Americans wear cowboy hats? No, that's a **stereotype**.

   a. an accurate cultural description   b. an overly simple cultural description

9. Kevin is a nice guy, but I can't **tolerate** his habit of interrupting every time I speak.

   a. allow; put up with   b. change something

10. Christina was invited to her friend's wedding on the same day as her brother's graduation. Of course, her family **took precedence**.

    a. was less important   b. was more important

B PERSONALIZE Discuss these questions with a partner.

1. If you were asked to give a brief **overview** of your culture's values, what would you say?

2. Which rules are **enforced** in your school or workplace? Which are not enforced?

3. What **stereotypes** exist about your own country? Is there any truth in them?

REFLECT   Analyze potential areas of difficulty in communication.

Before you read about cross-cultural communication, discuss these questions in a small group.

1. Are children in your culture taught to speak with respect to (a) older people and/or (b) those in positions of power?

2. You have an opinion that is very different from those of your classmates and teacher. Do you feel comfortable expressing this opinion to your classmates? To your teacher?

3. You have a disagreement with a coworker or classmate. What steps will you take to resolve the problem?

A woman in Tokyo, Japan, demonstrates her own style. Some cultures embrace individuality more than others.

COMMUNICATION
ACROSS CULTURES

A PREVIEW Look at the graph and answer the questions with a partner.

1. What do you think the characteristics being compared mean?

2. What cultural differences can you see between the citizens of the United States and those of Japan?

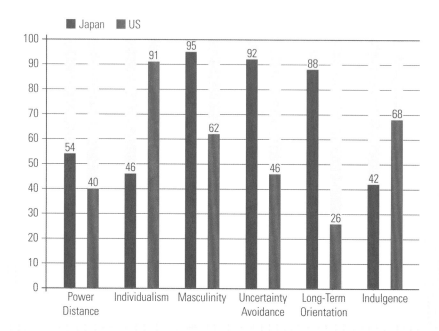

■ Japan ■ US

Power Distance · Individualism · Masculinity · Uncertainty Avoidance · Long-Term Orientation · Indulgence

🔊 **7.2** *Sometimes, cultural differences in communication lead to misunderstandings at work or at school, even though there are no problems with language.*

1   A large, multinational company has employees from many different countries. While they enjoy working together, they sometimes have a sense that something has been misunderstood, that they don't agree on the best approach to a task, or that a meeting has not gone as planned. Could their cultural backgrounds play a role in these communication difficulties?

2   Geert Hofstede (1928–2020) was a researcher in intercultural communications, who spent decades investigating how people around the world communicate in the workplace and in education. He came up with a number of "dimensions"—criteria by which the values of a culture are expressed. His research proposes an **overview** of the communication preferences of over 100 cultures around the world.

3   **Dimension 1: Power distance index (PDI)**

Do people accept inequality within their society? Some cultures have clear divisions between different levels; others are much more equal.

▶ In high-PDI cultures, it's more common to use family names and titles with those in higher-level positions. In low-PDI cultures, first names are common.

▶ In high-PDI cultures, decisions are often made by the person in charge; those in lower positions follow orders. In low-PDI cultures, the opinions of people lower down are taken into consideration.

▶ In high-PDI cultures, nonverbal forms of communication, such as bowing or standing up when a higher-status person enters the room, are more common.

4   Dimension 2: Individualism vs. collectivism (IDV)

Do people focus on themselves or on the group to which they belong? In an individualist culture, individual needs come first, while in a collectivist culture, loyalty to family or community **takes precedence**.

▸ Members of collectivist cultures are less **inclined to** disagree publicly with others. It's more important to maintain harmony within the group. Students, for example, may be reluctant to disagree with their classmates.

▸ In collectivist cultures, it's important not to embarrass others. A boss or teacher should not criticize someone publicly. The person will feel shame for disappointing his or her group.

▸ In individualist cultures, individual privacy is respected. It's understood that people may not want to share personal information with their colleagues.

5   Dimension 3: Masculinity vs. femininity (MAS)

Are historically masculine values, such as competition and **authority**, preferred? Are money and career success admired? Or does the culture embrace historically feminine values, such as **empathy** toward others?

▸ People in cultures that Hofstede describes as "feminine" may be more open to collaboration than those in Hofstede's "masculine" cultures, where competition is valued.

▸ Where a conflict arises, members of feminine cultures are often more willing to compromise and negotiate. Members of masculine cultures might be more eager to fight for what they want.

▸ In masculine countries, academic achievement is praised. In feminine cultures, weaker students are also celebrated. A school in a feminine culture may give a prize for the "kindest student" or the "student who made a contribution to school life."

6   Dimension 4: Uncertainty avoidance index (UAI)

To what extent do people value predictability and control over their lives? In high-UAI cultures, laws are established and **enforced**. In low-UAI cultures, there is a more relaxed attitude to life. Different ideas and approaches to life are **tolerated**.

▸ In education, students from high-UAI cultures like to know exactly what they are going to study and how they will be evaluated. Those from low-UAI cultures don't mind when a course is changed to meet students' needs.

▸ Teachers in high-UAI cultures are reluctant to admit that they don't know something. In low-UAI cultures, teachers who say "I don't know" are more readily accepted.

▸ In the workplace, high-UAI cultures have many rules their employees should follow, whereas low-UAI cultures are more flexible.

7   Dimension 5: Long- vs. short-term orientation (LTO)

Does the culture value tradition, or is it open to change? Cultures with long-term orientation are less willing to look at new ideas than those with short-term orientation.

▸ Company managers in cultures with long-term orientation are more likely to expect profits 10 years in the future, whereas those in cultures with short-term orientation want to get rich tomorrow.

► Members of cultures with long-term orientation form long-term connections with other people. There is a commitment to helping each other over a period of many years.

► In cultures with short-term orientation, people are expected to adapt to change quickly.

8 **Dimension 6: Indulgence[1] vs. restraint[2] (IVR)**

How important is it to enjoy life? People in high-indulgence cultures want to have fun. In contrast, high-restraint cultures are more likely to put personal needs aside to get the job done. Following social **conventions** is more common in these cultures.

► Meetings in high-indulgence cultures can be fun, with laughter and jokes. On the other hand, it's often best not to bring humor into a meeting in a high-restraint culture, but to focus on the purpose of the meeting.

► In education, students from cultures that value indulgence like to play games and have fun in class. Those from cultures that value restraint may see these activities as a waste of time.

► Members of high-indulgence cultures value their leisure time when they are not at work or in school.

9 **Criticisms of Hofstede's dimensions**

While Hofstede's work has led to an increased awareness of cultural differences in communication, it hasn't escaped criticism. The main criticism of Hofstede's model is that it's overly simplified and reduces vastly different people to **stereotypes**. It's impossible to **generalize** and to say that all Chinese, Brazilians, Saudis, Germans, or Americans are completely the same or different when it comes to communication. It's important to remember that every culture is made up of individuals, all of whom have different ways of communicating. The theory also ignores the fact that people are mobile today: They travel, they marry partners from other parts of the world, and they identify with more than one culture.

10 What do you think? Do you think Hofstede's dimensions are oversimplified and represent stereotypes? Or do they shed light on common communication problems in multicultural settings?

[1]**indulgence** (n) enjoying something that brings pleasure
[2]**restraint** (n) control over one's emotions and desires

B MAIN IDEAS Write the dimension addressed in each question.

a. _____ Which is more important: the person or the group?

b. _____ To what extent does the culture value tradition and growth over a long period of time?

c. _____ Are there clear divisions between higher and lower levels in society?

d. _____ Is having fun seen as important, or is it a waste of time?

e. _____ Is it important to have control over one's life?

f. _____ Does the culture value competition and success, or does it value kindness and collaboration?

C DETAILS Match each speaker to the Hofstede culture type they might come from.

a. Individualist   c. High indulgence   e. High power distance

b. Low uncertainty avoidance   d. Femininity   f. High uncertainty avoidance

1. _____ "I told a joke in a meeting today. I thought it was funny, but no one laughed. They all looked annoyed."

2. _____ "I emailed my teacher and addressed her as 'Professor.' She told me to call her Annie. I was shocked. I don't think that's polite."

3. _____ "We don't always agree, but surely we can compromise and reach an agreement we're both happy with."

4. _____ "My professor admitted today that she didn't know the answer to a question. I don't think she's very good. Maybe I'll change to a different class."

5. _____ "My coworkers keep asking me about my income, my family, even whether I plan to get married! I don't want to share that kind of information."

6. _____ "I enjoy the relaxed environment at work. As long as I get my work done, it doesn't matter what I wear, or what time I eat lunch."

CRITICAL THINKING   **Consider the limitations of research claims**

When you read research that makes bold conclusions, especially about human behavior, it is important to stop and think before generalizing. If someone says X happens because of Y, consider if there are other factors that can cause Y. For example, when you read about Hofstede's cultural dimensions, did you think, "This could be a cultural difference, but it might also happen because of the individual's personality, or because of the situation"?

REFLECT   Examine reasons for communication breakdowns.

Work in a small group. Read the following situations. For each one, decide:

▸ How would Hofstede explain this breakdown in communication? What went wrong?

▸ Could there be other reasons, such as personal or other noncultural factors, that explain why this situation happened?

1. Marta has been appointed director of her company's overseas branch, which is going through a difficult time. Marta arranges a meeting with everyone in the office to get their thoughts on how the company could be more successful. Her employees simply stare at her. No one says a word.

2. Leo is teaching a class of students from various cultures. On the first day, he tells his students that he doesn't have a detailed plan; he wants to "see how it goes" and figure out what to do from there. Leo later learns that some of his students have requested a different teacher as they think he is disorganized.

WRITE

UNIT TASK Write a compare-contrast essay about communication.

You are going to write a short essay about either the similarities or the differences between two aspects of communication. Use the ideas, vocabulary, and skills from the unit.

A MODEL Read the essay. Underline the three similarities discussed in the essay.

Spoken Languages and Sign Languages: A Comparison

1 There are about 6,500 languages in the world, and each one has its own system of sounds, words, and sentence structure. However, one group of languages is unique in that users of these languages do not use sounds to express thoughts. These languages are sign languages. They rely mainly on hand gestures to transmit meaning and are used mostly by the deaf. While the lack of sounds has led some people to wonder whether these are "real" languages, it is now widely accepted that sign languages such as American Sign Language (ASL) are languages like any other. They share several features with spoken languages: They have clear grammar rules; they include regional and social variation; and they can be used to express creativity.

2 First, both spoken languages and sign languages have systems of grammar. Spoken languages have grammatical ways of forming plurals, verb tenses, and questions; in the same way, sign languages also make use of grammatical rules. For example, users of spoken English form plural nouns by adding -s to the word. Users of ASL have several ways to make a noun plural, including using a word like "many" or repeating the sign. Users of spoken English indicate time by changing the verb form. Users of ASL imagine a line from behind the body to the front of the body; the position of a sign along this line indicates the time of the event. Users of spoken English ask a *yes/no* question by adding a form of the verb "do" ("Do you like chocolate?"); users of ASL keep the word order the same and indicate a question by raising their eyebrows. From these examples, we can see that sign languages assign signs for specific grammatical purposes, just as spoken languages do with words and parts of words.

3 Second, both spoken languages and sign languages show regional and social variation. Anyone listening to spoken English will notice differences between the English spoken in England and the English spoken in Ireland, Australia, or India. Speakers from each of these places may have difficulty understanding each other. In the same way, there are over 140 different sign languages around the world, including those found in Japan, Spain, China, Brazil, Thailand,

and more. In the English-speaking world, along with ASL, there are Australian Sign Language (AUSLAN), New Zealand Sign Language (NZSL), and British Sign Language (BSL), and users of one sign language cannot necessarily understand the others. Like spoken languages, sign languages also have idioms and slang terms, which are used by specific groups in society, such as teenagers. A common example is the use of signs for "train–go–sorry," which means "I'm not going to repeat what I just said." A sign language user might also sign "think–disappear" to suggest that he forgot something.

4   Finally, both spoken languages and sign languages are used for creative works. The English language is full of creative works, ranging from Shakespeare's plays to J. K. Rowling's novels. Similarly, there is a growing interest in the use of sign languages to create works of literature, including poetry and plays. They are filmed and performed live at cultural festivals, and several deaf theater groups have been founded around the world. One common theme for deaf creators is the idea of being part of a minority group. Unlike creative works in spoken languages, the works produced by deaf artists are not written down as there is no written version of these languages. In this way, deaf artists are continuing a long tradition of oral storytelling around the world, with the difference that their stories are passed on with their hands rather than their voices.

5   It is clear, then, that sign languages are not just simplified ways of using the hands to convey basic thoughts. Like spoken languages, they are highly evolved, complex forms of communication that can be used for both functional and creative purposes. For these reasons, sign languages are certainly "real" languages in every way.

A group of friends communicate using sign language.

B ANALYZE THE MODEL Work with a partner to outline the essay.

Title		
Introduction	Background	
	Thesis statement	
First body paragraph	Topic sentence	
	Supporting ideas/Details	
Second body paragraph	Topic sentence	
	Supporting ideas/Details	
Third body paragraph	Topic sentence	
	Supporting ideas/Details	
Conclusion	Final thought	

WRITING SKILL   Compare and/or contrast

When you compare and contrast two items, you are writing about their similarities and/or differences. Comparing and contrasting are common in academic writing. You might be asked, for example, to compare two historical events or two approaches to marketing. Here are some tips to keep in mind:

1. Focus mostly on either similarities or differences. Your thesis statement should briefly state what these are.
2. Each body paragraph should focus on only one specific similarity or difference with examples and analysis.
3. Support your points with statistics and other evidence. Avoid generalizations and stereotypes, especially if you are writing about groups of people.
4. Use signal words and phrases.

   To show similarity:
   > *A is . . .; similarly, B is . . .*
   > *A is . . .; In the same way, B is . . .*
   > *A is . . .; B is also . . .*

   To show difference:
   > *A is . . .; on the other hand/in contrast, B is . . .*
   > *While/Whereas A is . . ., B is . . .*

C NOTICE THE GRAMMAR Read the excerpt from the model and notice the underlined phrases. Work with a partner and note the reasons you think the article *the* is or is not used with these nouns and noun phrases.

There are about 6,500 languages in <u>the world</u>, and each one has its own system of sounds, words, and sentence structure. However, one group of languages is unique in that <u>users of these languages</u> do not use sounds to express thoughts. These languages are <u>sign languages</u>. They rely mainly on <u>hand gestures</u> to transmit meaning and are used mostly by <u>the deaf</u>.

1. the world _____

2. users of these languages _____

3. sign languages _____

4. hand gestures _____

5. the deaf _____

GRAMMAR   Articles to refer to groups

You already know that you should use *a* the first time you mention an item, and you should use *the* for subsequent references to that item. When you refer to a general group, such as people from a specific country, or people in a specific profession, or any other general group of people, animals, or things, follow these rules.

If you use a plural noun to refer to a group *in general*, do *not* use an article:

▸ ***Canadians*** *have a reputation for being welcoming to **people** from other countries.*

▸ *Research has shown that **women** often know more words for colors than **men** do.*

If a noun phrase (e.g., adjective + noun) is for a general group or idea, do not use an article:

▸ ***Masculine cultures*** *value authority and competition.*

▸ ***Bilingual people*** *sometimes feel that they have two personalities.*

If a noun phrase refers to groups in a <u>specific</u> situation, you can use *the*, but it is not always required. Often there will be a piece of information that makes the situation specific:

▸ ***The male participants*** <u>in the study</u> *responded differently from the female participants.*

▸ ***The Japanese students*** <u>at the university</u> *have established a social club.*

If you only use an adjective to describe a general group or idea, use *the*:

▸ *Many sign languages have been developed for use by **the deaf**.*

▸ *What can be done to help **the homeless**?*

D GRAMMAR Choose the better option in these sentences. Explain your choice to a partner.

1. **Coach / The coach** of the university football team is at practice every day.
2. Mercedes wants to work with **elderly / the elderly** after she graduates.
3. **Feminine cultures / The feminine cultures** value collaboration in the workplace.
4. **Students / The students** need to be careful when emailing their professors.
5. Are **artists / the artists** and **poets / the poets** always emotional, or is that a stereotype?
6. **Women / The women** in my class work harder than **men / the men**.
7. Edward enjoys learning **foreign languages / the foreign languages**.
8. **Chinese / The Chinese** invented the first paper money.

E GRAMMAR Write sentences about your culture. Share them with a partner and explain your use of articles.

Write three sentences about general groups in your culture.

▶ _____

▶ _____

▶ _____

Now, write three sentences about specific groups in your culture or community.

▶ _____

▶ _____

▶ _____

F EDIT Read the paragraph. Find and correct five errors with articles.

English Writing and Chinese Writing: An Overview

It has often been said that writers from different cultures organize the essays in different ways. In 1966, researcher Robert Kaplan found that the speakers of English write in a very direct way. There is a thesis statement at the beginning, and everything in the essay supports the thesis statement. In contrast, the Chinese traditionally use a style that is less assertive and more indirect, with the main idea often stated at the end. Whereas English writers try to present an individual point of view, the Chinese writers are thought to prefer ideas that reflect the opinion of their group. Of course, Kaplan's ideas are now quite old, and the world has changed. Researchers have provided evidence to suggest that his ideas are the generalizations and are not true for all the writers.

PLAN & WRITE

G BRAINSTORM Work in a small group. Choose two topics to compare. They can be two different languages or dialects; the language spoken by two different generations; written and spoken language; language use by men and women; or another related topic. Identify the similarities and differences between the two.

Topic	Similarities	Differences

H RESEARCH Follow the steps.

▸ Choose one topic from activity G and research it. Which ideas can you analyze and support with evidence? Which ones might be difficult to discuss without using stereotypes?

▸ Decide whether your essay will emphasize similarities or differences.

I OUTLINE Complete the outline.

Title _____

Introduction

    Background information _____

    Thesis _____

Body paragraph 1

    Main similarity or difference _____

    Supporting ideas/Details _____

    _____

Body paragraph 2

    Main similarity or difference _____

    Supporting ideas/Details _____

    _____

Body paragraph 3

    Main similarity or difference _____

    Supporting ideas/Details _____

    _____

Conclusion

    What can be learned from your analysis? _____

J FIRST DRAFT Use your outline to write a first draft of your essay.

K REVISE Use this list as you write your second draft.

- ☐ Did you give basic information about the two things you are comparing/contrasting?
- ☐ Did you make it clear whether you are focusing on similarities or differences?
- ☐ Did you include one specific idea supported with details in each paragraph?
- ☐ Did you avoid stereotypes and generalizations?
- ☐ Did you include only relevant information?

L EDIT Use this list as you write your final draft.

- ☐ Did you use the article *the* or no article correctly when referring to groups?
- ☐ Did you vary your use of words?
- ☐ Did you use different signal words for comparing and contrasting?

M FINAL DRAFT Reread your essay, expand on any unclear ideas, and correct any errors. Then submit it to your teacher.

A group of friends talking over breakfast.

REFLECT

A Check (✓) the Reflect activities you can do and the academic skills you can use.

- ☐ consider the relationship between language and thought
- ☐ evaluate ideas about language and thought
- ☐ analyze potential areas of difficulty in communication
- ☐ examine reasons for communication breakdowns

- ☐ write a compare-contrast essay about communication
- ☐ annotate a text
- ☐ compare and/or contrast
- ☐ articles to refer to groups
- ☐ consider the limitations of research claims

B Write the vocabulary words from the unit in the correct column. Add any other words that you learned. Circle words you still need to practice.

NOUN	VERB	ADJECTIVE	ADVERB & OTHER

C Reflect on the ideas in the unit as you answer these questions.

1. What was the most important thing you learned in the unit?

_____

_____

2. What have you learned about your own culture's communication style?

_____

_____

3. Which communication style would you like to learn more about? Explain why.

_____

_____

MAKE THE RIGHT CHOICE

Dr. Odette Doest, a veterinarian who runs a wildlife rehabilitation center on the island of Curaçao, with Bob, a flamingo she helped after it was injured.

CONNECT TO THE TOPIC

1. Why are Odette and Bob in a classroom?

2. Ethical issues are matters of right and wrong. In what situations might it be difficult to decide what is right and what is wrong?

An iceberg off
the coast of
Greenland

ETHICAL DECISION MAKING

A How is making a decision similar to an iceberg? Discuss the question with a partner. Now watch the video. Was your answer correct? ▶ 8.1

B Watch again. Match each driver of decision making to a possible result. ▶ 8.1

1. _____ Unconscious thoughts

2. _____ Unthinking custom and practice

3. _____ Ethical decision-making profile

4. _____ Reflective practice

a. We may be influenced by the beliefs of our family, friends, or colleagues, without ever questioning these beliefs.

b. We consider all aspects of the decision. We follow our purpose, values, and principles.

c. We may let biases influence our decisions, or we may ignore ideas that don't support our way of thinking.

d. We may be focused on outcomes or on relationships. We may ignore other important issues.

Complete the sentence with a number (1–4) from above:

We like to think we are most strongly influenced by number _____. In reality, we are most likely to be influenced by the other three.

C PERSONALIZE When was the last time you had to make an important decision? Which of the concepts in the video influenced your decision?

PREPARE TO READ

A VOCABULARY Complete the sentences with the correct form of the words.

acquire (v)	detrimental (adj)	integrity (n)	strategic (adj)	violate (v)
compatible (adj)	diminish (v)	reputation (n)	ultimate (adj)	widespread (adj)

1. The _____ luxury in a hotel is your own private swimming pool.

2. The company made a(n) _____ decision to close its smaller factory and move all operations to the main site to reduce delivery costs.

3. My team is struggling to win games. We need to _____ more players who can score goals.

4. Cathy decided to walk to school every day to save money. Her enthusiasm for this plan was _____ when the weather turned cold.

5. Diana and Angela shared an apartment, but they were not _____. Diana was quiet and tidy, while Angela liked loud music and was messy.

6. You can't photocopy the whole book! You'll be _____ copyright laws.

7. Professor Norton has a(n) _____ among her students for having high standards but also for being fair to everyone.

8. The government has tried to fight corruption in businesses and financial institutions, but the problem is still _____.

9. Silvio posted a negative comment about his company on social media. His actions were considered _____ to the company, and he was given a warning.

10. The mayor is a woman of _____. She always follows her high moral standards.

REFLECT Analyze whether actions are ethical.

You are going to read about actions that may be ethical or unethical. Discuss these questions in a small group.

1. Think of a story in the media that suggested that someone acted in an unethical way. What happened? Do you agree that they were unethical? What is your opinion about this person now?

2. Describe an action that would not be ethical in your school or college. Why is it considered unethical? Do you think this is the same in most other schools?

3. Can you think of any situations in which acting in an unethical manner, perhaps by cheating, can be considered acceptable?

ETHICS IN BUSINESS, TRAVEL, AND SPORTS

8.1 *Ethical considerations play a role in many decisions we make in life. As we work, travel, and enjoy leisure time, we may encounter situations that test our beliefs about right and wrong behavior. Read to learn about examples of ethical choices people have had to make in these contexts.*

Business

1   A woman was working as a social media manager for a school district in the United States. After learning that a storm was coming, one student posted online, "close school tammarow PLEASE." The woman responded by posting, "But then how would you learn to spell 'tomorrow' :)" She was ordered to delete her post and apologize to the student. She was then fired.

2   There are many cases of employees losing their jobs for something they have posted on social media. In some cases, the posts are related to their jobs. A worker at a child care center posted, "I just really hate being around a lot of kids." She was told not to come back to work. A server in a restaurant did not receive a tip for a $735 takeout order, and she complained on social media, naming the organization that had placed the order. She was fired. In other cases, offending social media comments are not related to the poster's job but are still not considered **compatible** with the employer's values. A mathematics teacher was fired for posting pictures of herself at a party, displaying behavior that her school did not consider acceptable. A public relations executive tweeted a racist comment before boarding an 11-hour flight to South Africa to visit her family; her tweet went viral[1], and by the time she landed, she had been fired.

---

[1]**go viral** (v phr) to attract a great deal of attention on social media

A PREVIEW Answer the questions.

1. What actions might get someone fired in the workplace?

2. Are there some destinations that tourists should not visit?

3. In professional sports, what actions might be considered unethical?

3   Reactions to these firings are mixed. Some people argue that an individual's social media posts are private, especially when they are not related to the job. Other people point out that many companies have codes of conduct: behavioral guidelines which employees should follow. Anyone who **violates** a code of conduct risks damaging the **reputation** of the company. Either way, the danger of social media use is clear: Think carefully before you post.

The beaches of Bali, Indonesia draw thousands of tourists every year.

You decide: When is it ethical and unethical to fire an employee because of their social media activity? Does it matter whether the post was written about the job or whether it was a personal post?

Travel

4   Antarctica has often been called the **ultimate** travel destination for nature lovers, and the number of tourists attracted by this wild, dramatic scenery is growing. In the 2018–2019 tourist season, over

56,000 people visited the continent. However, travel to the world's most extreme continent has an environmental impact, which has people questioning whether tourism there is ethical.

5   Those in favor of Antarctica tourism argue that travelers to Antarctica are so impressed by their visit that they spread the word about climate change and the need for environmental protection. There are also economic advantages to the tourist industry: Most travelers start their journey in towns like Ushuaia in Argentina or Punta Arenas in Chile, bringing economic growth to those places.

6   However, one study has found that damage to Antarctica's environment can occur with just 20 footsteps. There is a risk of introducing bacteria from outside into this fragile environment, which endangers plant and animal life. There is also a high risk of oil spills from the ships that bring tourists to the continent. As travel writer Costas Christ argues, "We could be just an oil spill away from destroying the pristine[2] environment we marvel at." But perhaps the biggest danger posed by travel to Antarctica is the journey to get there. Every tourist produces 4.4 tons of carbon dioxide (CO_2). CO_2 causes global warming, the single greatest threat to Antarctica.

7   Similar arguments are made about travel to other remote parts of the world. Consider the beaches of Bali, Indonesia; the shores of Lake Titicaca, Bolivia; the dramatic mountains of India—all have experienced a rapid increase in tourism over the last few decades, and all are threatened by overdevelopment and pollution. Many visitors to these regions go to admire incredible views but end up being distracted by garbage left from tourists.

You decide: When is it unethical to travel to parts of the world that are environmentally fragile? What can we do to make tourism like this more ethical?

Sports

8   At the 2012 Olympic Games in London, four teams in badminton were disqualified from the competition for "not using best efforts." In other words, they deliberately tried to lose a game.

Why would a competitor at the Olympics try to deliberately lose? The four teams had enough information about previous results to know that losing their last game in the opening round would be beneficial. It would ensure that they would meet a weaker opponent in the next round. When they were disqualified, they argued that they had made a **strategic** decision; if they hadn't tried to lose, they would have met a stronger opponent.

9   The practice of deliberately losing a sports game is known as "tanking," and it is **widespread**. Some managers of sports teams encourage their players to deliberately end the season in a low position. While the highest-finishing teams aim for the glory of winning a championship, the teams with the most losses have the best chances of **acquiring** the best new, young players for the next season. As such, there are many who think the worst place to finish a season is in the middle. Tanking has been called "an open secret"—it happens frequently, but hardly anyone admits to it. One exception is an owner of a National Basketball Association (NBA) team who admitted publicly that he had encouraged tanking. He was fined $600,000 for making public statements that were "**detrimental** to the NBA."

10   The problem is not limited to the NBA: Other professional sports leagues have had cases of teams tanking late in a season. Many do not agree that this is a reasonable option. Opponents of tanking say it **diminishes** the principle of fair play, which states teams should always play to win, and the best one should win. It is also unfair to fans, who pay to see a competitive match with an unknown outcome. Lawyer and ethics advisor Sally Afonso says, "Any coach or manager [who] encourages this is demonstrating unethical leadership and impairing the **integrity** of the game itself."

You decide: Is tanking an acceptable strategy or a violation of fair play? What should be done by professional sports leagues regarding this issue?

---

[2]**pristine** (adj) unspoiled; not polluted

B MAIN IDEAS Match each dilemma with the correct example from the reading.

1. _____ Individual freedom of speech vs. company reputation
2. _____ Economic growth vs. environmental conservation
3. _____ Strategic planning vs. integrity

a. Should tourism be allowed in certain parts of the world?
b. Is tanking an acceptable practice?
c. What social media use is acceptable and unacceptable?

C DETAILS Choose the *incorrect* piece of information.

1. The article talks about the following unethical social media practices:
   a. Complaining online that you don't like your job
   b. Sharing company secrets, such as new products
   c. Posting negative remarks about other people

2. Why does travel to Antarctica raise questions about ethics?
   a. The environment in Antarctica is easily damaged.
   b. There is a chance of introducing bacteria to the continent.
   c. Tourists might run into danger and need to be rescued.

3. What are the main complaints against teams who deliberately lose games?
   a. They won't have the opportunity to acquire new players.
   b. It goes against the principle that the best team should win.
   c. The fans will not be happy.

Tourists in the mountains of India

READING SKILL   Identify arguments and counterarguments

When you read about a matter of right and wrong, notice arguments and counterarguments to determine if the text is balanced. A text that presents only one side of an argument may not be looking at the whole picture. On the other hand, if the author acknowledges both sides of the issue, and explains why one position is stronger than the other, the argument is more complete and convincing. As you read persuasive pieces, identify the writer's main arguments. Try to predict any counterarguments that might be made, and ask yourself whether the author acknowledges these. This will allow you to decide how complete the author's argument is.

D APPLY Review the main ideas of the reading. In your notebook and in your own words, state the counterarguments provided for each of the following arguments. Compare your ideas with a partner.

1. It doesn't matter what I post on social media in my own time and from my own phone. That has nothing to do with my work.

2. Travel to fragile places should be discouraged; the risk to the environment is too great.

3. If we deliberately lose this game, we'll get an advantage in the next round. It's a good strategy.

E APPLY Read the opinions and write a counterargument for each.

1. I'm considering becoming a vegetarian. Some of my friends who have stopped eating meat say they feel much healthier and have so much more energy.

   Counterargument: _____

   _____

   _____

2. I've also heard that not eating meat could save me a lot of money. I could buy enough groceries for a week without spending much money.

   Counterargument: _____

   _____

   _____

3. But the main reason why people don't eat meat is for ethical reasons. People say that it isn't ethical to eat animals when there's so much else that we can eat.

   Counterargument: _____

   _____

   _____

CRITICAL THINKING   Understand bias

Everyone has an opinion about ethical issues, and often there is no "correct" or "incorrect" position. In many cases, someone's opinion can be traced to personal background: culture, education level, age, gender, profession, and social connections. If that person presents only one side of an argument because of personal interest, this is known as *bias*. Recognize how bias affects your own opinions and those of others so that you can make informed decisions, separating personal beliefs from reasoned arguments.

F   APPLY Read the situation. Then complete the table with a partner and decide which group you both would agree with and why.

As a natural region with very little pollution, the Rocky River area attracts increasing numbers of people from the city who come in search of a quiet life. The region is also home to a variety of wildlife. However, there are plans to build a new airport in the region. The residents have different opinions on this.

Opinion	Who might say this?	How might bias affect their opinion?
It will be great for the region.		
It will be a disaster. We can't let this happen.		

REFLECT   Evaluate situations and make ethical decisions.

Work in a small group and discuss how you might respond to each of the following situations. Give reasons for your responses.

1. Your colleague, Jack, is looking for a new job. He has asked you not to tell anyone. Jack has recently been given a promotion, and he now has access to a lot of confidential information about your company. Would you tell your boss?

2. You discover that some money is missing from your hotel room. You suspect the housekeeper. You have chatted with her, and you know that one of her children is sick and needs medicine. Would you discuss this with hotel management?

3. You learn that the captain of your soccer team has been offered a sum of money to lose a game. You know you should tell someone, but the captain has recently become engaged to your cousin and will be joining your family. What would you do?

PREPARE TO READ

A VOCABULARY Use one of the words to replace the underlined word or phrase in each sentence.

compensation (n)	consent (n)	justify (v)	stimulus (n)	undergo (v)
conform to (v phr)	intervene (v)	sequence (n)	trauma (n)	withdraw (v)

1. If you don't like a class in college, and you think you made the wrong choice, you can <u>leave</u>. _____

2. Wendy was arrested for stealing food from the supermarket. She tried to <u>explain the reason for</u> her action by saying it was for her elderly parents. _____

3. Jo and Alex could not work together; they were always arguing. In the end, the boss had to <u>become involved</u>, and she moved Jo to another department. _____

4. At what age can people in your country get married without their parents' <u>permission</u>? _____

5. The car accident caused Patrick to experience long-term <u>pain and suffering</u>. _____

6. Yasmin broke her leg at work when she slipped on a wet floor. Her company gave her <u>money for the harm she had suffered</u>. _____

7. Airline pilots are required to <u>take part in</u> regular checks of their mental and physical health.

8. The police asked the suspect about the <u>series</u> of events that led to the crime. _____

9. Ken went to work wearing clothes that did not <u>follow</u> his company's code of conduct regarding dress. He was told to go home to change his clothes. _____

10. Restaurants are often decorated in bright colors, such as red and orange, because they are thought to be a <u>way of making people want</u> to eat a large meal. _____

REFLECT Consider ethics in experiments.

You are going to read about ethics in experiments involving young people. Discuss the questions in a small group.

1. Can you think of any cases in which the behavior of children or young adults was studied? Were there any ethical issues in these cases?

2. What does the expression "The end justifies the means" mean? In what situations might this expression be applicable or not applicable when it comes to experimenting on humans?

LEARNING FROM HISTORY'S MISTAKES

The Stanford Prison
Experiment, 1971

A PREVIEW Look at the photo and answer the questions.

1. What do you think is happening in this photo?

2. What ethical questions come to mind as you look at this photo?

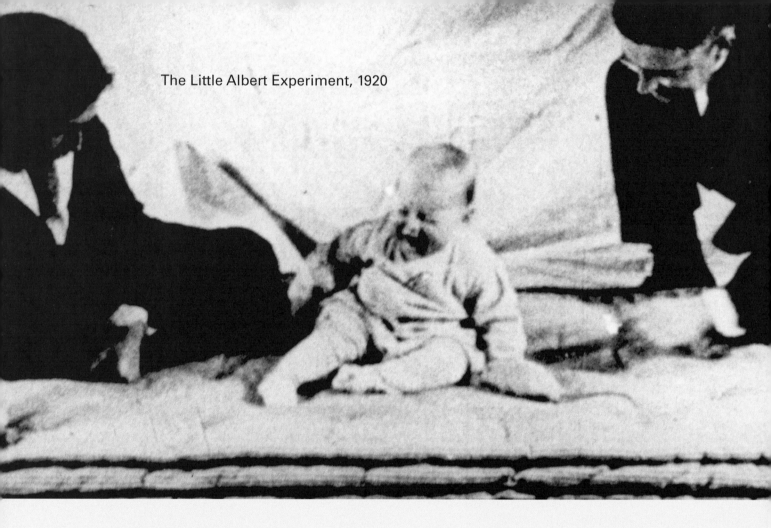

The Little Albert Experiment, 1920

1   Anyone wishing to undertake research with human subjects today must ensure that their procedures are ethical. There are several sets of guidelines that govern research with humans; all are based on three main principles:

▶ Participants (or their parents, in the case of children) must give their **consent** to take part in the experiment, and they must be allowed to **withdraw** from the study at any time.

▶ The research should maximize benefits for the participants and for society, while minimizing risks for both.

▶ During the research, the participants should be treated in a way that is respectful and protects their well-being.

2   Unfortunately, this was not always the case. In the past, researchers either lacked awareness of modern ethical standards or were guided by the belief that the end **justifies** the means. The three experiments outlined here, which all involved children and young adults, are shocking in the ways they do not **conform to** today's ethical guidelines.

The Little Albert Experiment

3   Little Albert was a nine-month-old child who **underwent** a series of tests in 1920. At that time, Ivan Pavlov had already shown that dogs could be trained to show a specific emotional response when presented with a **stimulus**. When Pavlov rang a bell and provided food, the dogs became excited and produced saliva[1]. Later, when Pavlov rang a bell, but did not provide food, the dogs still produced saliva; they had learned to associate the sound of the bell with the presence of food. Researcher John Watson wanted to find out whether the same could be true of humans.

4   In the first of a **sequence** of tests, Albert was shown a series of animals, including a dog, a monkey, a rabbit, and a white rat. Albert showed no fear.

---

[1]**saliva** (n) a liquid produced in the mouth when food is present

Next, the white rat was again shown to Albert. Albert liked the animal and wanted to play with it. Once the researchers had established a positive reaction to the rat, they moved to the next stage. Now, when Albert reached for the rat, a metal bar behind his head was hit with a hammer to make a loud noise. The noise scared Albert, and he cried. This happened several times, until Albert came to associate the presence of the rat with the unpleasant noise.

5   The result was that every time Albert was shown the rat, he cried, even when no noise was made. He had become afraid of an animal he had previously liked. Furthermore, he went on to exhibit a fear of other animals, including a dog and a rabbit, as well as a mask worn by the researcher, and a fur coat. Albert had been taught to be afraid of ordinary objects that had similar characteristics to the rat.

6   There is no information about whether the experiment had a long-term effect on Albert. However, the experiment has been criticized for possibly causing mental harm to a small child by creating **trauma** through the use of animals. Clearly, Watson's data on infant responses to stimuli were not worth the pain caused to this child.

The Monster Study

7   In 1939, Wendell Johnson and his research assistant, Mary Tudor, carried out an experiment designed to determine the effects of positive and negative feedback on children's use of language. The researchers found 22 children in an orphanage[2] and told them they would be given help with their speech. Ten of these children had stutters[3] and other speech difficulties; the others did not.

8   The children were divided into two groups. Each group had children with and without speech difficulties. The children in the first group were all praised for their use of language; they were told that they *did not* have a stutter, that any difficulties were temporary, and that they would outgrow any problems. Those in the second group, on the other hand, were told that they *did* have a stutter; they were reminded to self-correct; and they were told: "Don't ever speak unless you can do it right."

9   This treatment had an effect on the speech of the children in the second group. Of the six non-stutterers, five actually started to stutter, and of the five who already stuttered, three became worse. More importantly, the study had a huge effect on their mental well-being. The children who received negative feedback experienced long-term trauma. They became self-conscious and reluctant to speak; this lasted for much of their lives. The experiment was named the "monster study" by the participants, several of whom received a public apology and financial **compensation** later in life.

The Stanford Prison Experiment

10   In 1971, 12 young men were arrested, blindfolded, and taken to a prison, where they were introduced to 12 guards. The prisoners were given prison clothing, had chains placed around their ankles, and were identified by numbers rather than by their names.

11   This was no normal prison. The "criminals" and "guards" were actually students at Stanford University, California, and the "prison" was in the basement of a university building. Researcher Philip Zimbardo remembers, "I was interested in what happens if you put good people in an evil place." He built a realistic "prison" on campus, with advice from former prisoners, and he advertised for students to take part in the experiment for $15 per day.

12   The guards had been given instructions to do whatever was needed to maintain order, with the exception of using physical violence. They very quickly found other ways to assert[4] their authority. They deprived the prisoners of food and sleep and made them do physical exercise in the middle of the night. They forced the prisoners to wear bags over their heads, and they limited prisoners' use of the bathroom.

---

[2]**orphanage** (n) an institution for children whose parents are dead or unable to care for them

[3]**stutter** (n) a speech difficulty in which the speaker finds it hard to say a whole word

[4]**assert** (v) to do something to show power

13 The prisoners soon exhibited signs of suffering, including crying and screaming. Two needed to be removed from the experiment; another initiated a hunger strike⁵ to be allowed to leave. Several of the prisoners contacted their parents and asked them to **intervene**, for example, by contacting lawyers. Both prisoners and guards seemed to have forgotten that they were simply taking part in an experiment and could withdraw at any time.

14 The experiment was intended to last for two weeks. It was called off after only six days, when Zimbardo's friend, also a researcher, visited the site and was shocked by the suffering she saw. She told Zimbardo, "Young boys are suffering, and you are responsible." Six days were enough for Zimbardo to reach his conclusion: In the right circumstances, good people can do bad things.

15 In all three studies, the researchers had good intentions: They wanted to learn more about the human mind. However, they all raise the dilemma of how far researchers can go in experimenting on humans. All three studies have been widely criticized on ethical grounds for the psychological distress inflicted on the participants. Today, with ethical guidelines in place for researchers, none of these experiments would be allowed to happen. The responsibility now is with researchers to try to gather the data they need without causing harm to humans or animals in the process.

---

⁵**hunger strike** (n) the refusal to eat in order to achieve a goal

B MAIN IDEAS Answer the questions.

1. Why are the experiments in the reading considered to be unethical?

   _____

   _____

   _____

2. What is the author of the article's position with regard to human experimentation? What statements tell you this?

   _____

   _____

   _____

   _____

3. What do researchers need to do today? _____

   _____

C DETAILS Complete the table to summarize each of the experiments.

	Little Albert Experiment	Monster Study	Stanford Prison Experiment
Research Question			
Researcher(s)			
Participant(s)			
Methodology			
Ethical Concern			

D DETAILS Which of these statements can you infer from the article? Write Y for *Yes* or N for *No.*

1. _____ Albert quickly forgot the trauma he had experienced.

2. _____ Most researchers in the 1930s worked with children from orphanages.

3. _____ Criticizing a child with a physical difficulty can change that child's personality.

4. _____ The Monster Study participants resented Johnson for a long time.

5. _____ The Stanford Prison "guards" were troubled young men who wanted to hurt others.

6. _____ Philip Zimbardo was surprised by the students' behavior.

REFLECT Apply ethics to an experiment.

Imagine you are a researcher planning an ethical version of the Stanford Prison Experiment. Like Zimbardo, you want to find out how humans react when placed in positions of power and/or subordination. Keep the guidelines at the beginning of the reading in mind and write answers to these questions in your notebook. Then compare answers in a small group.

▸ In what ways can you design a similar study but prevent mental distress?
▸ What would you do differently from the original experiment? List three changes you would make.

WRITE

You are going to comment on an ethical dilemma and write at least one response to others on a discussion board. A discussion board is an online "bulletin board" where you leave comments and can expect to see responses from members of your class. If you cannot set up an online discussion board for this assignment, you can complete the task in a small group in class on paper or on a computer.

A MODEL Read the online discussion. As you read each student's contribution, consider whose arguments you think are the strongest and why.

Discussion Board

Instructions: Read the dilemma below. Post your response on the class discussion board, referring to other students' ideas whenever possible. Be sure to do the following:

▸ Write clearly and persuasively. Use specific supporting information.
▸ Engage with other students by responding directly to their ideas.
▸ Be polite and respectful, especially when disagreeing with a classmate.
▸ Check your grammar, spelling, and punctuation.

Your friend Jessie is a medical student in her first year. She has recently taken her first exam in anatomy and scored 68 percent—not great, but not too bad. Most of her classmates scored between 60 and 70 percent. However, Tyler scored 95 percent. Jessie was impressed and a little envious, until she overheard Tyler talking on the phone. He was describing a complex method he had used to cheat on the exam. Jessie has asked you what she should do.

Lin: OK, I'll start. There's no doubt in my mind that Jessie should report Tyler. Academic integrity is such a big topic these days. Everyone knows cheating is wrong. Schools, colleges, and universities make this very clear to all students. There is no excuse for not knowing it's wrong. Just look at our own university handbook. There are 10 pages about academic dishonesty. If I had cheated on my last exam, I would have gotten a better grade, but I wouldn't have been proud of myself, and I probably would have been caught. Tyler CANNOT BE ALLOWED to get away with this. It isn't fair to students who study and don't cheat. He probably won't be expelled, and his medical career won't be over, but he'll learn an important lesson.

Marcus: I see your point, Lin, and obviously Jessie needs to do something. However, let's look at the big picture for a moment. It's the first exam, and Tyler was probably nervous. Maybe his parents are making financial sacrifices to send him to medical school, and he doesn't want to let them down. I know how that feels. My parents used all their savings to send me here. Maybe he acted in a way that is not in his true nature because he was scared. Let's not be so quick to judge him. I think Jessie should talk to him, tell him what she knows, and see if she can get him some help. Maybe an appointment with a counselor would help, and their services are confidential.

Ami: I agree with Marcus. Tyler might have some personal issues. He might be under a lot of stress. If he talked to a professional, he would get some advice on how to approach his studies. The university has great support services he can use for free. They can be very helpful, and they won't tell anyone. Everyone deserves a second chance. Haven't you ever made a mistake? I think Jessie should offer Tyler some friendly advice and encourage him to get some help.

Lin: If I understand you correctly, Ami, you're saying that Jessie should give Tyler a gentle reminder that cheating is unethical and suggest he get help. Are you serious? We don't even know what his issues are. Everyone has personal issues to deal with, but we learn to cope, and we don't cheat on tests. This guy is going to be a doctor! He can't get away with this. We can't have doctors cheating on tests. He'll either end up incompetent, or he'll go through his career cheating on everything. He cheats in medical school, and 10 years later, he's cheating by overcharging patients or by not paying his taxes! Listen, my grandfather is a well-known cardiologist. If he'd cheated in medical school, he wouldn't be successful today—he would have been expelled. I can't believe anyone would have any sympathy for this cheat!

Ami: Lin, you say that Tyler is going to be a doctor, and he can't be allowed to cheat. That's true, but shouldn't his friends be more supportive? Jessie can urge him to get counseling now, at an early stage in his medical career. Maybe a few sessions with a counselor would help him figure out why he acted in this way. Maybe the problem can be solved before it gets too serious. A counselor could help Tyler understand why he resorted to cheating. Or maybe he'll realize that medicine is not the right career for him. Either way, he'll be helped rather than punished.

Natasha: Tyler cheated on a test, so there should be consequences. It's a very serious offense, especially for someone in a position of trust, like a doctor. If I knew my doctor had cheated in medical school, I would be uncertain about her abilities to take care of my health. A lot of people don't trust doctors. On the other hand, Tyler might be under pressure from his family, so we need to support him. I think he should talk to a counselor.

B ANALYZE THE MODEL Work with a partner and assign each student a score from 1–4 (1 = lowest; 4 = highest) for their contribution according to the teacher's instructions. Who has the highest overall score, and why?

	Write clearly and persuasively. Use specific supporting information.	Engage with other students by responding directly to their ideas.	Be polite and respectful, especially when disagreeing with a classmate.
Lin			
Marcus			
Ami			
Natasha			

WRITING TIP

When communicating online, be aware of the tone of your message. Keep in mind that you cannot rely on facial expressions, gestures, or laughter to show you are not upset or angry when using strong, direct language. It's very easy to read direct language as rude or aggressive, especially during a debate. Therefore, always reread your online communication and ask yourself: How would I feel if someone wrote this to me?

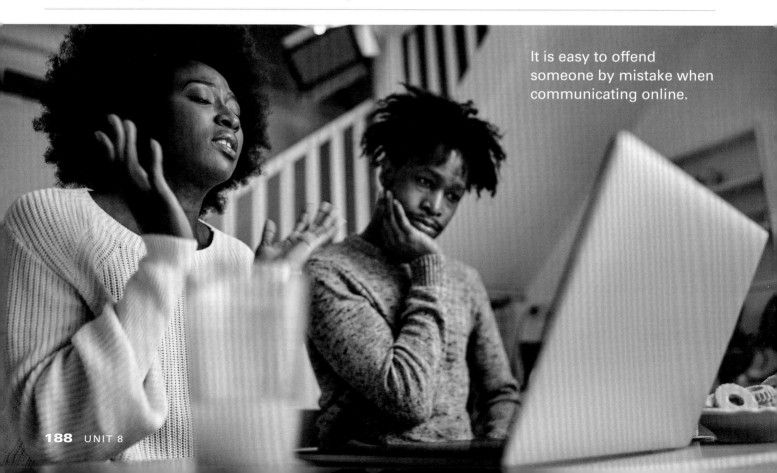

It is easy to offend someone by mistake when communicating online.

WRITING SKILL   Write persuasively on a discussion board

To participate in a discussion board, you need to do the following:

▶ Respond to the question being asked, following the instructions you are given and using supporting details to make your opinion clear.

▶ Respond to other people's comments, showing you have considered them.

▶ Write in a clear, convincing, and respectful manner.

Here are some tips to keep in mind:

1. Be concise. Make your point clearly and directly. Don't include irrelevant information.

2. Add to the conversation. Don't simply repeat what other students have written.

3. Be respectful of other people's opinions. Avoid saying negative things about other people.

4. Break up a long response into paragraphs. A large block of text is hard to read.

5. Avoid distractions that hurt your credibility. Fix all spelling and grammar mistakes. Don't use emoticons or text-message language. Don't use all CAPITAL LETTERS.

6. Use language such as this:

    To agree with someone's post

    I think that's a good point, especially as . . . [add something new]

    I agree. There's another reason why . . . [add something new]

    To disagree politely

    I see what you're saying, but I think . . . [add counterargument]

    That [detail about other person's post] is true, but what about . . . [add counterargument]

    To question someone's post

    If I understand you correctly, you're saying . . . [paraphrase original post]

    Do you mean . . . [share your understanding of the original post]

C NOTICE THE GRAMMAR Complete the sentences with the correct form of the verb given. Check your answers by reviewing the model. Then work with a partner and discuss why these verb forms are used in these sentences.

1. **Lin:** If I _____ (cheat) on my last exam, I _____ (get) a better grade, but I _____ (not be) proud of myself—and I probably _____ (be) caught.

2. **Lin:** If he _____ (cheat) in medical school, he _____ (not be) successful today—he _____ (be) expelled.

3. **Natasha:** If I knew my doctor _____ (cheat) in medical school, I _____ (be) uncertain about her abilities to take care of my health.

GRAMMAR   Unreal conditionals

Use these different types of conditionals to write about:

Present action or situation with imagined or unreal future result

if + were/simple past   would/might (not) + verb
If I **were** sure what to do in this situation, I **would do** it.

if + were/simple past   would/might (not) + verb
If you **asked** 20 students to take part in an experiment for money, they **might** all **agree**.

Past action or situation with imagined or unreal past result

if + had (not) + past participle   would/might (not) have + past participle
If I **had known** you were feeling stressed, I **wouldn't have shouted** at you.

would/might (not) have + past participle   if + had (not) + past participle
She **wouldn't have gotten** compensation **if** she **had not been hurt**.

Past action or situation with imagined or unreal present result

if +   had (not) + past participle   would/might (not) + verb
If the doctor **had not suggested** the experimental treatment, my brother **might not be** alive today.

would/might (not) + verb   if + had (not) + past participle
I **would not be living** in Tokyo **if** I **hadn't gotten** this job offer.

D GRAMMAR Complete the sentences with the correct form of the verb given.

Several students at Central College are considering their course choices:

1. If I _____ (not like) math so much, I _____
   (not study) engineering. I'm glad I did.

2. If someone _____ (tell) me that Statistics 101 was so difficult,
   I _____ (not take) that course. I wish I had known!

3. If I _____ (pass) my chemistry course, I _____
   (apply) to medical school. Sadly, I failed it.

4. If I _____ (choose) to do a graduate degree,
   I _____ (investigate) the ethics of global tourism. It could have been an
   interesting career.

5. I really regret the choices I made. If I _____ (study) business,
   I _____ (have) a good job today.

E GRAMMAR Complete the sentences in your own words, using correct verb forms.

1. If John Watson had continued to work with Little Albert, _____

_____

2. If Albert's parents had witnessed the experiment, _____

_____

3. If Wendell Johnson had not had access to children in an orphanage, _____

_____

4. If the children had known the real purpose of the experiment, _____

_____

5. If Zimbardo's friend had not visited the site, _____

_____

6. If the Stanford students had been too distressed to continue their studies, _____

_____

F EDIT Read the paragraph. Find and correct four errors with the grammar.

Blue Eyes, Brown Eyes

In 1968, a teacher named Jane Elliott carried out a controversial experiment with her students. She divided the children, aged eight and nine, into two groups: those with blue eyes and those with brown eyes. She announced that the brown-eyed children were more intelligent and worked harder than the blue-eyed children; this was the result of genetic differences. After a short time, the blue-eyed children started to make mistakes in their work, and they were treated unkindly by the brown-eyed children. Jane Elliott's goal was to show the effects of discrimination on the basis of color. Today, over 50 years later, her exercise is met with mixed reactions. Some people say that she caused psychological harm to the children. If they didn't undergo this experiment, they hadn't felt bad about themselves then and possibly after the experiment. On the other hand, many people admire her. They say that if the children have not taken part in the activity, they might not have learned about discrimination. They might even grown up with negative feelings toward people of different races. Which side do you agree with? How would you have felt if you had been a blue-eyed child in Jane Elliott's class?

PLAN & WRITE

G CONSIDER THE DILEMMAS With a group, choose one of the dilemmas.

Dilemma A:

Neil is the editor of his campus newspaper. He needs to hire a photographer. This is a voluntary position, but the successful candidate will be gaining valuable work experience. He has received two applications. Nahid is a very skilled photographer who has submitted an impressive portfolio of her work. Patricia's work is less developed, but Patricia is Neil's cousin. He knows that she works hard, she is a strong team player, and she has a lot of talent. Neil thinks she deserves this opportunity. He has asked you which candidate he should choose.

Dilemma B:

You are voting for the head of student government at your university. Martina is a candidate, and you know her since you are in some classes together. She has strong leadership skills, she is an excellent communicator, and you think her ideas are creative and exciting. However, you have heard rumors that she is unkind to people she doesn't like, excluding them from social events and even posting mean messages about them on social media. You're not sure whether to vote for Martina as your representative.

H BRAINSTORM When you have chosen a dilemma, spend a few minutes on your own, thinking about different arguments and counterarguments. Take notes in your notebook. Then decide which position you want to take and brainstorm ideas for supporting it.

I POST Use your notes to write your first post either on an online discussion board or a piece of paper. If groups choose different dilemmas, you will need a separate discussion board for each. Use this list to check your post.

- ☐ Did you make your point clearly and concisely?
- ☐ Did you support your ideas with logical examples and reasons?
- ☐ Did you write in a tone that is respectful to others?
- ☐ Did you avoid distractions, such as long blocks of text, language errors, and very informal writing?

J RESPOND Monitor the discussion board to see who has replied. When others comment on your post, follow up with one or more suitable responses. If you are not working in an online discussion board, give your paper to another group member to respond. Consider these questions as you write your responses.

- ☐ Did you respond respectfully, first showing you understand the other point of view with an appropriate tone?
- ☐ Did you continue the conversation by addressing previous points and adding new ideas?

REFLECT

A Check (✓) the Reflect activities you can do and the academic skills you can use.

☐ analyze whether actions are ethical

☐ evaluate situations and make ethical decisions

☐ consider ethics in experiments

☐ apply ethics to an experiment

☐ write persuasively on an ethical question

☐ identify arguments and counterarguments

☐ write persuasively on a discussion board

☐ unreal conditionals

☐ understand bias

B Write the vocabulary words from the unit in the correct column. Add any other words that you learned. Circle words you still need to practice.

NOUN	VERB	ADJECTIVE	ADVERB & OTHER

C Reflect on the ideas in the unit as you answer these questions.

1. What was the most interesting thing you learned in the unit?

   _____

   _____

2. Has this unit inspired you to reconsider any choices you have made in the past or to change your opinion on any news story you have heard about in the media? Explain.

   _____

   _____

3. What was your favorite topic from this book? Explain why.

   _____

   _____

Using a dictionary Choosing synonyms

Synonyms are words that are similar in meaning. Though similar, many have slightly different uses. The verbs *make* and *construct*, for example, both mean *to form or build*, but they are not interchangeable: You would *make a cake* but *construct a building*. *Construct* implies a more complicated building task.

The definitions and sample sentences in a dictionary can help you decide the most appropriate use of words with similar meanings.

A Choose the best word to complete each sentence. Use a dictionary as needed to understand which choice is most appropriate.

1. The food bank program was (**prosperous / successful**). It provided food for 500 families in need.

2. The plan was (**naive / simple**). It could never work.

3. What is the (**ethical / right**) choice for this dessert: chocolate or vanilla?

4. In an effort to (**launch / start**) her campaign, the candidate scheduled several interviews.

5. They found the (**funding / money**) in a bag behind the market.

6. His problematic behavior made him a(n) (**example / role model**) of how <u>not</u> to act in school.

7. The (**maintenance / preservation**) of cultural heritage is important.

8. In order to (**increase / maximize**) space in my small apartment, I bought folding chairs.

9. Computer (**learning / literacy**) is a required skill in most fields today.

10. Good communication is important to effectively (**collaborate / cooperate**) with your peers.

B Rewrite each sentence, replacing the word in bold with a synonym. Use a dictionary if necessary.

1. Please **cover** your answers so that no one can see them.

   _____

2. She's **disappointed** because she was not able to raise enough money.

   _____

3. There are too many **cars** on the road.

   _____

4. Be sure to put your **garbage** in the correct container.

   _____

5. I hope you are able to **achieve** your goals.

   _____

6. He is **popular** because he is always so kind.

   _____

Root words

Many words in English are formed by taking basic words and adding affixes (prefixes and suffixes). Many of these basic words are built from Greek or Latin roots. For example, *cycle* is made from the root word *cycl* which comes from the Greek for "circle." Knowing the meaning of root words can help you understand unfamiliar vocabulary.

A Match the words from Unit 2 (1–5) with the correct definition (a–e).

1. chronic
2. consumption
3. contradict
4. disturbance
5. interfere

a. to tell someone what he or she says isn't true
b. a break in the peace or quiet
c. to get in the middle of a situation
d. the process of eating, drinking, or using things
e. long-lasting

B Match the root words (1–5) with the correct meaning (a–e). Use the definitions in activity A to help you.

1. chron
2. sump
3. dict
4. turb
5. inter

a. to stir up
b. between, among
c. time
d. to say, to speak
e. to take, to use

C Use the root words to guess and write the meanings of the words in bold. Then check your answers in a dictionary.

1. The months of the year happen in **chronological** order.

_____

2. **Turbulence** can make a plane ride very bumpy.

_____

3. Your phone's charger is **interchangeable** with mine.

_____

4. The results are not in yet, but the **assumption** is that she will win.

Formal and informal language

In professional and some academic situations, you are likely to use more formal language. In casual or more personal situations, you often use less formal language. The words you choose can show this difference.

More formal: She **regretted** her mistake.

More informal: She **felt sorry about** her mistake.

Notice that in formal language, you often use multisyllable single words (such as "regretted") more than in informal language. You also don't often use spoken expressions and multi-word phrases (such as "felt sorry about") as often.

A Match the informal word(s) in bold with the formal word (a-f). Check your answers in a dictionary.

1. He is a **really great** piano player. _____
2. Her professor was her greatest **supporter**. _____
3. He is a **good** employee. _____
4. Her feelings about her work were **strong**. _____
5. The researchers **took note of** the changes. _____
6. Research assistants **helped with** the project. _____

a. competent
b. perceived
c. accomplished
d. intense
e. advocate
f. facilitated

B Choose the more formal word or phrase to complete each sentence.

1. There is a **probability / good chance** that the economy will grow next year.
2. Some users report that the new phone is a **better / superior** product than the old version.
3. Experts suggest you do your homework early—don't **put it off / procrastinate**.
4. Early humans **lived in / inhabited** the area we now call Africa.
5. Scientists found that the new drug **mitigated / lessened the amount of** the patients' **long-lasting / chronic** pain.

C Write sentences using three of the formal words from activities A and B.

_____

_____

_____

Using a dictionary Building word families

You can change some verbs to nouns and adjectives by adding a suffix. Common adjective suffixes are *-ive, -ent, -cal, -ing, -ed*. Common noun suffixes are *-ment, -tion, -ence, -ity*.

A dictionary often includes different forms of a word as separate entries. Sometimes a dictionary will list other forms of the word after the definition of the most common form. For example:

> **active** *adj.* 1 doing things that require physical movement 2 involved in a group or organization *-v.* **act**; *-n.* **action**; *-adv.* **actively**

A Use a dictionary to find other words in the same word family.

Verb	Noun	Adjective	Adverb
		collective	
		comparative	
		consistent	
		effective	
exaggerate			
manipulate			—
	stability		—

B Write sentences about yourself. Use the correct form of the words in bold.

1. (verb form of **comparative**) _____

_____

2. (noun form of **consist**) _____

_____

3. (noun form of **exaggerate**) _____

_____

4. (adjective form of **manipulate**) _____

_____

5. (verb form of **stability**) _____

_____

Prefixes *con-, col-, com-,* and *cor-*

The prefix *con-* means "with" or "together." For example, to *connect* something means to join together. The prefix *con-* can sometimes be spelled *col-, com-,* or *cor-.* Follow the rules below:

con- is used with root words beginning with most consonants   *consume*

col- is used with root words beginning with *l*   *collaborate*

com- is used with root words beginning with *b, p,* and *m*   *communicate*

cor- is used with root words beginning with *r*   *correlate*

A Add the correct prefix to each word.

1. To make pancakes, first _____bine eggs, flour, milk, and oil in a bowl.

2. Scientists often _____laborate on research projects so that they can share their findings.

3. Your phone is made from hundreds of tiny _____ponents.

4. The study shows that smoking and stress _____relate to lower life expectancy.

5. There is _____sensus among scientists that climate change is real.

6. People like living in a _____munity that is safe.

7. The photo has an interesting _____position.

8. The word *blonde* _____locates with hair but not with furniture.

B Match the words in activity A to the definitions below.

1. _____: (v) to show a close similarity between two things

2. _____: (n) an agreement with a group of people

3. _____: (v) to work together

4. _____: (v) to go together with

5. _____: (n) parts that make something when put together

6. _____: (n) a place where people live together

7. _____: (n) an arrangement

8. _____: (v) to mix together

Using a dictionary Choosing the correct meaning

Many words have two or more meanings. Use a dictionary to check the different meanings. Each entry uses a numbered list to show the different definitions. For example, there are two main meanings for *acceptance*. Use context clues to determine the correct meaning.

acceptance *n.* **1** favor, approval: *His work received acceptance by his peers.* **2** the act of accepting: *She received an acceptance for admission to college.*

A Write the best definition for the bold words. Use the context and a dictionary to help.

1. The **collapse** of the financial markets in 2008 caused misery for millions.

   _____

2. Prices of phones have **declined** in recent years.

   _____

3. The virus was believed to have been **transmitted** from bats to humans.

   _____

4. With the money that she won, she **speculated** in the stock market.

   _____

5. A **prominent** issue in climate change discussions is how to reduce the use of fossil fuels.

   _____

6. After many years, he finally **accepted** that he was not going to be a professional soccer player.

   _____

7. The president gave an **address** to other leaders at the United Nations.

   _____

8. After the game, the crowd **filtered** slowly out of the stadium.

   _____

9. After high school many students **pursue** a college degree.

   _____

10. People donated money toward the **foundation** of a new hospital wing.

   _____

Collocations *Take* + noun

Collocations are two or more words that often go together. It's useful to learn collocations the way you learn individual words. Here are some common collocations with the verb *take* + noun:

take account (of): to consider, note
take advantage (of): to make good use of something
take charge (of): to have control
take effect: to start, to become valid
take issue (with): to object to something
take part (in): to participate
take shape: to form, to develop
take stock (of): to reflect on the current situation before making a decision

A Choose the correct noun to complete each sentence. Two words are extra.

account	advantage	charge	effect	issue	part	shape	stock

1. Many people take _____ with politicians who say climate change isn't real.

2. When my parents are away, my big sister takes _____ and tells us what to do.

3. The plan didn't take _____ of the weather; the rain delayed everything by two days.

4. You need to wait several minutes for some medicines to take _____.

5. During the meeting, the design for the new website starting to take _____.

6. Jeans were on sale last week. I took _____ and bought two pairs.

B Complete the sentences using the correct form of a collocation from activity A. Use your own ideas.

1. Recently, I _____

2. Last year, someone I know _____

3. The world would be a better place if _____

4. During the summer I _____

5. One problem I often have is _____

Compound words

A closed compound word is formed when two words are joined together to make a new word. For example, *lifetime* is a closed compound word. Some closed compound words are joined with a hyphen, for example *check-in*. Open compound words (*high school*, *living room*) are not joined together but are still considered compound words.

Sometimes, it's possible to guess the meaning of a compound word from its two parts. For example, *well-known* means famous. Other compound words are harder to guess. Use the context to guess the meaning, then check in a dictionary.

A Guess the meaning of the compound words in bold. Then match the words to the correct meanings (a–f).

a. land with farms, trees, and a few houses	c. pride in oneself	e. take back what was said
b. a person of little ability or intelligence	d. detailed look	f. not cooked enough

1. _____ The chicken was **underdone** so we just ate the salad.

2. _____ The company **backtracked** on the plan to move to another city. It now says it will stay in its current location.

3. _____ The magazine took a **close-up** of the latest situation in the country.

4. _____ Many schools teach kids **self-respect** so that they grow up to have a healthy opinion of themselves.

5. _____ The **countryside** around San Francisco is a beautiful place to explore.

6. _____ Some colleagues thought he was smart, others though he was a **lightweight**.

B Match the parts of the compound words together. Check your answers in a dictionary.

1. wide-_____   a. pack

2. bed _____   b. new

3. after _____   c. eyed

4. back _____   d. minded

5. brand-_____   e. room

6. open-_____   f. noon

VOCABULARY INDEX

*Academic words

VOCABULARY INDEX

TIPS FOR READING FLUENTLY

Reading slowly, one word at a time, makes it difficult to get an overall sense of the meaning of a text. As a result, reading becomes more challenging. In general, it is a good idea to first skim a text for the gist, and then read it again more closely so that you can focus on the most relevant details. Use these strategies to improve your reading speed:

- ▶ Use section headings, as well as the first and last lines of paragraphs, to help you understand how the text is organized.
- ▶ Read groups of words rather than individual words.
- ▶ Keep your eyes moving forward. Read through to the end of each sentence or paragraph instead of going back to reread words or phrases.
- ▶ Use clues in the text—such as bold words and words in italics—to help you know which parts might be important and worth focusing on.
- ▶ Skip structure words (articles, prepositions, etc.) and focus on words and phrases carrying meaning—the content words.
- ▶ Use context clues, affixes, and parts of speech—instead of a dictionary—to guess the meaning of unfamiliar words and phrases.

TIPS FOR READING CRITICALLY

As you read, ask yourself questions about what the writer is saying. Think about why the writer is presenting the information in the text. Important critical thinking skills for academic reading include:

- ▶ **Analyzing**: Examining a text closely to identify key points, similarities, and differences.
- ▶ **Applying**: Deciding how ideas or information might be relevant in different contexts, e.g., applying possible solutions to problems.
- ▶ **Evaluating**: Using evidence to decide how relevant, important, or useful something is. This often involves looking at reasons for and against something.
- ▶ **Inferring**: "Reading between the lines," in other words, identifying what a writer is saying indirectly rather than directly.
- ▶ **Synthesizing**: Gathering appropriate information and ideas from more than one source and making a judgment, summary, or conclusion based on the evidence.
- ▶ **Personalizing/Reflecting**: Relating ideas and information in a text to your own experience and viewpoints.

TIPS FOR NOTE-TAKING

Taking notes will help you better understand the overall meaning and organization of a text. Note-taking also enables you to record the most important information for future use, such as when you are preparing for an exam or completing a writing assignment. Use these techniques to make your note-taking more effective:

- As you read, underline or highlight important information, such as dates, names, and places.
- Take notes in the margin. Note the main idea and supporting details next to each paragraph. Also, note your own ideas or questions about the paragraph.
- On a separate piece of paper, write notes about the key points of the text in your own words. Include short headings, key words, page numbers, and quotations.
- Use a graphic organizer to summarize a text, particularly if it follows a pattern such as cause-effect, compare-contrast, or chronological sequence.
- Keep your notes brief by using abbreviations and symbols like these.

approx. approximately	**Ch.** Chapter	**>** is more than
→ leads to / causes	**b/c** because	**<** is less than
e.g./ex. example	**p.** page; **pp.** pages	**~** is approximately / about
↑ increases / increased	**w/** with	**info** information
↓ decreases / decreased	**re:** regarding, concerning	**yrs.** years
i.e. that is / in other words	**w/o** without	**para.** paragraph
etc. and others / and the rest	**incl.** including	**excl.** excluding
& / + and	**=** is the same as	∴ therefore

TIPS FOR ACADEMIC WRITING

There are many types of academic writing (descriptive, argumentative/persuasive, cause-effect, etc.), but most types share similar characteristics. Generally, in academic writing, you should:

- write in full sentences.
- use formal English. (Avoid slang or conversational expressions such as *kind of*.)
- be clear and coherent—keep to your main point; avoid technical words that the reader may not know.
- use connecting words or phrases and conjunctions to connect your ideas.
- have a clear point (main idea) for each paragraph.
- use a neutral point of view—avoid overuse of personal pronouns (*I, we, you*) and subjective language such as *nice* or *terrible*.
- use facts, examples, and expert opinions to support your argument.
- avoid using abbreviations or language used in texting. (Use *that is* rather than i.e., and *in my opinion*, not *IMO*.)
- avoid starting sentences with *or, and*, or *but*.

CONNECTING WORDS & PHRASES

To give an opinion	To give examples	To link ideas/to add information
In my opinion, . . . I (generally) agree that . . . I think/feel (that) . . . I believe (that) . . . It is my personal view that . . .	An example of this is . . . Specifically, . . . For instance, . . .	Furthermore, . . . Moreover, . . . In addition, . . . Additionally, . . .

To present similar ideas	To present different/contrasting ideas	To give reasons
Similarly, . . . Both . . . and . . . Like . . . , . . . Likewise, . . .	However, . . . On the other hand, . . . In contrast, . . . Conversely, . . . Despite the fact that . . . Even though . . . Unlike . . . , . . .	This is because (of) . . . This is due to . . . One reason (for this) is . . . This is a consequence of . . . For this reason, . . .

To show results or effects	To describe a sequence	To conclude
Therefore, . . . As a result, . . . Because of this, . . . If . . . , then . . .	First (of all), . . . Then/Next/After that, . . . As soon as . . . Once . . . Finally, . . .	In conclusion, . . . In summary, . . . To conclude, . . . To summarize, . . .

To summarize/paraphrase	To analyze and critique a text	To explain a concept
Overall, the text argues that . . . The main point is . . . The author feels that . . .	The significance of . . . is . . . This is a good/poor example of. . . This is important because . . . This is a strong/weak argument because . . .	This is like . . . Think of this as . . . Essentially, this means . . . In other words, . . .

To refer to sources	To give evidence or present facts	To convey attitude
According to . . ., In the article . . ., . . . asserts/argues/claims/ states . . . We know from . . . that . . .	There is evidence/proof . . . Studies show . . . Researchers found ... . . . tells us/shows us/proves that . . .	Certainly, . . . Clearly, . . . Of course, . . . Sadly, . . . Surely, . . . (Un)Fortunately, . . .

INDEX OF EXAM SKILLS & TASKS

Reflect is designed to provide practice for standardized exams, such as IELTS and TOEFL. This book has many activities that focus on and practice skills and question types that are needed for test success.

Illustrations: All illustrations are owned by © Cengage.

Cover © Ben Mulder; **2–3** (spread) © Stephen Zeigler; **4** Thomas Imo/Photothek/Getty Images; **6–7** (spread) Alex Fradkin/Redux; **8–9** (spread) Ryan Carter/Alamy Stock Photo; **13** Diyana Dimitrova/Shutterstock.com; **16** RVillalon/Shutterstock.com; **18–19** (spread) kyoshino/E+/Getty Images; **14–15** (spread) nikkytok/iStock/Getty Images; **26–27** (spread) © Corey Arnold; **28** Paolo Woods and Gabriele Galimberti/National Geographic Image Collection; **30–31** (spread) Amy Dickerson/The New York Times/Redux; **31** © Cengage; **33** © Joshua Trujillo; **37** © Magnus Wennman; **38** © Cengage; **39** bymuratdeniz/E+/Getty Images; **48** David Trood/DigitalVision/Getty Images; **50–51** (spread) Sheng Li/Stringer/Reuters; **52** JHU Sheridan Libraries/Gado/Archive Photos/Getty Images; **54–55** (spread) © Lauren DeCicca; **57** © Lauren DeCicca; **61** Lillian Suwanrumpha/AFP/Getty Images; **62–63** (spread) Brent Stirton/Getty Images; **66** Peter Muller/Cultura Creative RF/Alamy Stock Photo; **74–75** (spread) © Samar Jodha; **76** hadynyah/E+/Getty Images; **79** © Cengage; **78** Danny Hu/Moment/Getty Images; **80** (tl) © Cengage, (b) Bettmann/Getty Images; **85** Universal History Archive/Universal Images Group/Getty Images; **87** David Sailors/Corbis Documentary/Getty Images; **89** © Cengage; **90** ventdusud/iStock/Getty Images; **93** Tjetjep Rustandi/Alamy Stock Photo; **98–99** (spread) © AKA Jimmy C; **100** Federica Grassi/Moment Open/Getty Images; **102–103** (spread) © Sisse Brimberg/National Geographic Image Collection; **104** Heritage Images/Heritage Image Partnership Ltd/Alamy Stock Photo; **105** © Dillon von Petzinger; **109** NurPhoto/Getty Images; **110** Cooter/Alamy Stock Photo; **114** © Ted Harrison; **122–123** (spread) Gerd Ludwig/National Geographic Image Collection; **124** Maja Hitij/Getty Images News/Getty Images; **128** © Cengage; **133** © Middle Usumacinta Archaeological Project/Takeshi Inomata; **135** Betsy Boynton, Dyncorp Systems & Solutions, contracted to the USGS. Public domain; **139** Editorial Image Provider/Universal Images Group/Getty Images; **142** Library of Congress Prints and Photographs Division Washington, D.C. 20540 USA; **126–127** (spread) Johannes Eisele/AFP/Getty Images; **131** Robert Postma/Solent News/Shutterstock.com; **146–147** (spread) Tim Graham/Hulton Archive/Getty Images; **148** Julie Edwards/Alamy Stock Photo; **150–151** (spread) © Carol Beckwith and Angela Fisher/Photokunst; **152–153** (spread) Alexandre Morin-Laprise/Moment/Getty Images; **157** Mark Kolbe/Getty Images News/Getty Images; **163** urbazon/E+/Getty Images; **168** Maskot/Getty Images; **170–171** (spread) Jasper Doest/National Geographic Image Collection; **172** posteriori/E+/Getty Images; **174–175** (spread) simonlong/Moment/Getty Images; **177** Yawar Nazir/Getty Images News/Getty Images; **181** © Dr. Philip Zimbardo; **182** Courtesy of Benjamin Harris; **188** FluxFactory/E+/Getty Images.